W0200200

MATURA-TRAINING

ENGLISCH

Lesen und Hören

Rainer Jacob • Paul Jenkinson

STARK

Autoren:
Rainer Jacob hat durch seine langjährige Arbeit als Englischlehrer, in der Lehrerfortbildung sowie als Schulleiter – z. B. an einer Auslandsschule in Lima / Peru – eine Fülle von sowohl praktischer Lehrerfahrung als auch theoretischer Kenntnisse vorzuweisen. Er veröffentlichte im STARK Verlag bereits Lernhilfen für unterschiedlichste Bildungssysteme und Schularten.

Paul Jenkinsons langjährige Berufserfahrung im Unterricht in deutschsprachigen Ländern wie auch in seiner Heimat Großbritannien ist ein wichtiger Garant für praxisnahe Englisch-Lernhilfen. Mit regelmäßigen Reisen in seine „alte Heimat" verschafft er sich immer wieder einen frischen Eindruck über die in englischsprachigen Ländern aktuellen Themen.

Umschlagbild: © bravobravo / iStockphoto

Inhalt

MP3-CD

Track 1: Life in the UK – Citizenship Test
Track 2: The hazards of overpopulation – Intro
Track 3: The hazards of overpopulation
Track 4: Inside the White House: The kitchen garden – Intro
Track 5: Inside the White House: The kitchen garden
Track 6: How government influences behaviour in society – Intro
Track 7: How government influences behaviour in society
Track 8: Taking the thug out of thug life – Intro
Track 9: Taking the thug out of thug life
Track 10: American icons: Georgia O'Keeffe's skull paintings – Intro
Track 11: American icons: Georgia O'Keeffe's skull paintings – Part 1
Track 12: American icons: Georgia O'Keeffe's skull paintings – Part 2

Autoren

Reading Comprehension: Rainer Jacob
Listening Comprehension: Paul Jenkinson

Vorwort

Liebe Maturantinnen und Maturanten,

seit 2015 gibt es die **standardisierte Reife- und Diplomprüfung**, die gemeinhin unter dem Namen „Zentralmatura“ bekannt ist. Hierbei rücken vor allem in den modernen Fremdsprachen die **Kernkompetenzen** noch mehr in den Fokus. In Englisch sind dies für die schriftliche Prüfung Lesen, Hören und Schreiben, in AHS kommt außerdem noch die Sprachverwendung im Kontext dazu.

Der vorliegende Trainingsband soll Sie auf zwei dieser vier geforderten Kompetenzbereiche vorbereiten – nämlich **„Reading comprehension“** und **„Listening comprehension“**. Der Band gibt Ihnen **Strategien und Tipps** an die Hand, wie Sie Ihre Fertigkeiten beim Lesen und Hören allmählich steigern können, um schließlich mit einem guten Gefühl und dem nötigen Rüstzeug versehen die Reifeprüfung zu bestreiten. Sie werden in den folgenden Kapiteln aktuelle, fordernde und interessante Texte zu vielen unterschiedlichen Themenbereichen vorfinden. Dazu erwarten Sie verschiedenste Aufgaben, mit denen Sie die Techniken der Texterschließung trainieren können und die sie **schrittweise an das Niveau der Matura heranführen**. Zu jedem Text gibt es auch mindestens eine **Übungsaufgabe im Stil der Matura**. Das Trainingsmaterial in diesem Band eignet sich für angehende Maturanten an AHS sowie BHS.

Im abschließenden **Lösungsteil** finden Sie nicht nur die Lösungen aller Aufgaben zur Selbstkontrolle, sondern auch weitergehende Hinweise und Hilfestellungen sowie die **Transkripte der Hörtexte**.

Die beiliegende **MP3-CD** enthält alle Hörtexte zum Kapitel „Listening“ – authentische Podcasts, Reden und Interviews zu verschiedenen Themen.

Wir wünschen Ihnen eine effektive Prüfungsvorbereitung und viel Erfolg in Ihrer Englisch-Matura!

Rainer Jacob

Paul Jenkinson

Allgemeine Hinweise

Englische Texte zu lesen und zu verstehen ist eine Herausforderung, die nicht nur in einer Prüfung gemeistert werden will, sondern auch in vielen Bereichen des privaten und beruflichen Lebens wichtig und entscheidend sein kann. Doch ist es mit dem „Durchlesen" eines Textes meist nicht getan. Gerade in der Prüfung wird von Ihnen verlangt, einzelne Aspekte eines englischen Textes herauszufiltern, die Aussage und Intention des Autors eines argumentativen Aufsatzes zu erkennen oder einzelnen Abschnitten eines informativen Artikels Teilüberschriften zuzuordnen.

Dieses Kapitel soll Sie mit diesen und noch weiteren Aufgabenformen vertraut machen und Ihnen dabei helfen, sich anhand interessanter, vielschichtiger Texte auf die **„reading comprehension"** der Zentralmatura-Klausur vorzubereiten. Dabei können und sollten Sie diesen Band als langfristige Hilfe bereits deutlich vor der unmittelbaren Prüfungsvorbereitung nutzen.

Aufbau des Leseverstehens in der Zentralmatura

Der Bereich **Lesen** besteht in der Prüfung aus **Aufgaben zu vier verschiedenen Texten** zu unterschiedlichen Themenbereichen. Es handelt sich um authentische Texte, zu denen in der Regel keine Vokabelangaben gemacht werden. Damit Sie für diese Prüfungssituation optimal vorbereitet sind, hilft Ihnen dieser Trainingsband, Ihren Wortschatz im Vorfeld der Prüfung zu erweitern. Als Hilfestellung finden Sie zu jedem Lesetext Erklärungen zu evtl. schwierigen oder unbekannten Wörtern. Außerdem werden zu Beginn jedes „Topics" Aufgaben gestellt, die für den jeweiligen Text relevante Vokabeln erklären und einüben. Am besten lernen Sie für Sie schwierige Vokabeln aus diesen Aufgaben sowie aus den „Annotations" konsequent mit, dann wird Ihnen sicher auch das Verständnis der Lesetexte in der Matura leichter fallen.

Aufbau der „Topics"

Die verschiedenen möglichen Aufgabenformen des Bereichs Leseverstehen werden im Folgenden eingehend erläutert und eingeübt. Dabei werden Sie **Schritt für Schritt** an die Aufgaben der Zentralmatura **herangeführt** und durch eine breitgefächerte Auswahl an „Topics" mit recht verschiedenen Themenbereichen konfrontiert.

Die einzelnen „Topics" sind wie folgt aufgebaut:

- **„Pre-reading activities"** dienen hauptsächlich der Vorentlastung des im Text verwendeten Vokabulars und bereiten zudem auf die Thematik des Textes vor. Diese Aufgaben nützen Ihnen am meisten, wenn Sie sie vor dem ersten Lesen des Textes bearbeiten.
- **„Understanding the text":** Diese Aufgaben erleichtern als Vorstufe die Bearbeitung der Aufgaben im Stil der Matura; sie zeigen Möglichkeiten auf, sich einem Text und seiner Bearbeitung in Teilschritten zu nähern. Hier werden Sie auch aufgefordert, den Text zum ersten Mal zu lesen.
- **„Matura-style tasks"** stellen mögliche Prüfungsaufgaben dar; der Umfang und die Schwierigkeit orientieren sich an den veröffentlichten Musteraufgaben des „Bundesinstituts für Bildungsforschung, Innovation und Entwicklung des österreichischen Schulwesens" (BIFIE). Die verschiedenen Aufgabentypen werden im Unterpunkt „Common reading comprehension tasks of the ‚Matura'" beispielhaft vorgestellt. Eine Übersicht, welcher Aufgabentyp in welchem „Topic" vorkommt, gibt Ihnen die Tabelle auf Seite 7.

Lösungsteil

Die Lösungen zu den Aufgaben stehen Ihnen – nach „Topics" geordnet – am Ende des Buches (im **„Key"**) zur Verfügung. Zusätzlich werden Ihnen Hinweise und alternative Lösungen angeboten. Versuchen Sie diese Möglichkeit der Vorbereitung zu nutzen, d. h. schauen Sie nicht bloß nach, ob Sie richtig oder falsch lagen, sondern verwenden Sie die Lösungen und die Hinweise, um zu überprüfen, warum etwas nicht richtig beantwortet wurde oder wie die Antwort zustande gekommen ist. Nur durch Fehler und deren gezielte Verbesserung können Sie diese abstellen und in der Prüfung vermeiden.

„Tips"-Kästen

Tips

In diesen Kästen, die in den „Topics" auftauchen werden, finden Sie **Hinweise zu den jeweiligen Aufgaben:**

- Sie sollen Ihnen **Strategien** vermitteln, wie Sie diese und auch ähnliche Aufgaben schneller und effizienter lösen können.
- Aufgabenformen, die Sie in der Matura erwarten, werden hier **Schritt für Schritt** erläutert.

Reihenfolge der „Topics"

Der **Schwierigkeitsgrad** der „Tasks" **erhöht sich** von „Topic" zu „Topic", sodass Sie sich allmählich steigern und an das Niveau der Reife- und Diplomprüfung gewöhnen können. Wir empfehlen Ihnen darum, die vorliegende

Reihenfolge der Aufgaben zu berücksichtigen. Dies ist auch deshalb ratsam, weil die zusätzlichen Tipps zu den Aufgaben („Tips"-Kästen) vor allem in den ersten „Topics" zu finden sind. In den letzten beiden „Topics" wird eine Kenntnis der Aufgabentypen bereits vorausgesetzt. Die Texte entsprechen in Länge und Schwierigkeitsgrad der Matura und decken zudem ein großes Spektrum von Themenfeldern ab, sodass Sie nicht nur Ihre sprachlichen Kompetenzen trainieren können, sondern auch Kenntnisse im Bereich Kultur und Landeskunde vertiefen können.

Bevor Sie jedoch mit der Bearbeitung der Aufgaben beginnen, sollten Sie unbedingt die folgenden Strategien und beispielhaften Beschreibungen der vorkommenden Aufgabentypen durchsehen, die Ihnen gute Dienste bei der Bearbeitung der folgenden „Topics" – und hoffentlich auch bei Ihrer Reifeprüfung – leisten werden.

However, as the following chapter should prepare you for the English test, let's continue in English …

Useful techniques and strategies in reading tasks

Before reading a text

The first impulse that students often follow when dealing with reading comprehension is to grab the text and read through it with hardly any aim – as if they just want to get quickly done with it. This might not be the best strategy.

Actually, the first thing you should do is to **read the task(s)** and/or the questions because you clearly want to know what you have to read a text for. Depending on what you are asked to do in the task, there are mainly two different methods or techniques of reading texts – both can be practised in the upcoming topics – which you should be able to perform in the "Matura": reading for the gist and reading for detail.

Reading for the gist

The "gist" is the **main line of thought of a text** and its author, which you can only get by reading the text as a whole. The general method is to **"skim" a text** – that means you do not read word-by-word, but you read faster than you normally do while trying to get a general overview of the text. In the topics and tasks ahead you will be able to try different ways of doing that. Use that practice in order to be prepared for any text showing up in the "Matura".

Reading for detail

The method of **"scanning"** a text for details should be used in tasks where you have to **focus on a special aspect of a text** or on specific information. Usually before doing so, you should know the general meaning, purpose or tone of a text, which may help you a lot. Then you should be able to focus on the relevant detail, which may be just one single piece of information that can only be found at a certain point within a text. Therefore, you should always check if you have understood the task – so that you don't look for the wrong or inappropriate piece of information.

Time management

Make sure that you choose one of those methods before dealing with a task. Reading a text without a purpose or trying to find too much in one reading session can cost you precious time in a test situation. One of the most important factors when dealing with examinations is your time management.

You should always arrange a certain amount of time for checking your answers after completing a question (and as far as this book is concerned: before looking up the key). That may also include reading the text again – even if you think you don't have to.

However, do not rush or lose your head while doing the exercises. Take your time, focus on the relevant tasks and the examination will work out well.

Common reading comprehension tasks of the "Matura"

Multiple Choice

This kind of task seems simple at first glance and some people even think that they have a good chance of guessing the correct answer. However, the chances of choosing an incorrect solution are even higher. There are often "distractors" (likely but wrong answer options) which are only distinguishable from the correct solution if you know the text in detail or when you have found the corresponding information within the text.

Example

Text (reference):
"Overnight a very odd and huge circle had appeared in one of his wheat fields. The corn had been neatly flattened into a large circular pattern [...] Farmer Jameson did not see any footprints, so he couldn't explain how the circle had got there." (Topic 4)

Task/Answer:
Farmer Jameson was surprised because ...

a) ☐ a huge spaceship had landed in his field.
b) ☒ he saw a huge pattern in his field.
c) ☐ his wheat field had been destroyed.
d) ☐ the corn in his wheat field had been cut overnight.

Tip: Always check the other options to make sure that you have really found the correct one. And don't think that the correct options' position follows a pattern ("Muster") or a logical order – for example, if you have "a, b, c, a, b, c, a" as correct options, then the next one does not automatically have to be "b". Look at every exercise as if it was the only one. However, if you cannot find the correct answer, it is better to guess a solution than to leave a blank, of course.

Matching

There are many different forms of matching tasks. In the "Matura" you may be asked to either "match sentence beginnings to their corresponding endings using information from a text", to "match headings to paragraphs in a text" or to "match sentences to gaps in the text". Be careful not to fall for the "distractors".

Example

Text (reference):

"To cover these offences a new word was coined: cyber crime or wire fraud. Cyber crime is the latest addition to the group called 'white-collar crimes' and represents one of the greatest threats to a country's national security, economic prosperity and public safety." (Topic 5)

Task: Match the corresponding parts of these sentences.

A The new term cyber crime …
B The well-being of the nation …
[…]

1 cannot be detected very easily by the police.
2 is in danger while this new type of crime becomes popular.
3 describes a special kind of criminal offence.
[…]

Answer:

A	B	…
3	2	…

Tip: Sometimes you might be able to rule out impossible answer options because they do not fit logically. Do so before reading the text and focus on the remaining options for every answer.

Gap filling/ Short-answer questions

The gaps are filled with a maximum of four words. The information that you need to answer the questions can be found in the text but you may have to use your own words. When filling in the gaps, keep as close to the text as possible.

Example

Text (reference):

"If you asked him [William] how many hours he works each day, he probably couldn't tell you exactly. […] There are no clocks in the mill, anyway." (Topic 3)

Task/Answer:

Why was William unaware of how long he worked every day?

no clocks in factory/mill

Tip: At first you must find the correct passage or sentence in the text. Then you have to rearrange the words or paraphrase them (use synonyms and/or your own words). Consider using short forms; they count as one word, not two. Usually there is more than just one possibility.

True/False with evidence

Here you have to do two things at once: find the corresponding sentence in the text where the information relating to the statement can be found and state if the statement is true or false. Give the first four words of the corresponding sentence in order to show that you found the correct passage within the text.

Example

Text (reference):
"Having often heard reports of legendary westward voyages [...], Christopher Columbus studied old books and charts to acquire more information."
(Topic 2)

Task/Answer:

Statement	True	False	First four words
a) Columbus based his voyage on the tales of other seafarers.	☒	☐	*Having often heard reports*

Tip: It is a good idea to highlight the corresponding section with a marker while scanning the text for the information.

Where to find "Matura-style" tasks

In the table below you can see in which topic you will find the different types of "Matura tasks":

Matura-style tasks	Topics ❶	❷	❸	❹	❺	❻
Multiple Choice	✗			✗		✗
Matching	✗			✗	✗	
Gap filling/Short-answer questions		✗	✗			✗
True/False with evidence		✗	✗		✗	

Advertising for kids

Text 1

0 In our digital age media consumption is steadily on the increase, with the Internet, social networks and television taking first place across generations. Psychologists and educators have often pointed out that children represent a particularly captive audience.

1 Recent studies in the USA reveal that young people aged 8 to 18 spend an average of more than seven hours daily using some kind of entertainment media. Consequently, all sorts of businesses, large and small, take advantage of the extensive media usage and spend enormous amounts of money targeting children with commercials. According to market researchers children aged 2–11 watch more than 25,000 advertisements a year on TV alone, a figure that does not include product placement and concealed advertising in TV shows and films.

2 There is general agreement that advertising is necessary because it helps firms to boost sales and thus generates jobs – not least in the advertising agencies which create the ads and commercials. In addition, it helps finance not only TV programmes, but also cultural and sporting events, many of which could not be staged without donations from industry. It goes without saying that the firms themselves profit to a certain degree from sponsoring by improving their image, but especially in the arts and entertainment sector the investment does not usually yield returns.

3 The food industry is one of the biggest spenders on the advertising market and has developed special strategies to market foods and beverages to children on television, on the Internet, on mobile phones, in magazines, through product placement in movies and video games. In addition, adverts appear on product packages, on clothing and other merchandise, and almost anywhere where a logo or product image can be shown, too.

4 More often than not, these advertisements have a greater influence on children's choice of food than what the parents tell their children to eat; especially the very young do not understand the persuasive intent of adverts and cannot distinguish between advertising and programmes. Parents complain that aggressive food marketers undermine their authority, because adverts give children a completely different view of what is healthy to eat.

Whereas parents would like their kids to stick to a nutritious diet by eating vegetables, fruit and salads, food adverts aimed at children mostly promote low-nutrition foods full of fat and sugar.

5 For a long time, the health authorities have appealed to food and beverage companies, stores, broadcasters and schools to market foods responsibly to children. This means that, above all, they should support parents' efforts to foster healthy eating habits in children, banning all adverts which might be harmful to the mental and physical health of the younger generation.

6 These appeals seem to be bearing fruit as a change in the advertising strategies of several major companies is taking place. In cooperation with the government and citizen action groups, they have worked out and agreed on guidelines for food marketing to children in order to avoid the negative effect on children's well-being. Fast-food chains, for example, have committed themselves to limiting advertising aimed at children younger than 12 to food and drinks that meet strict nutritional guidelines.

7 In addition, for children under 12 years old they will offer special Kids Meals that provide no more than 560 calories per meal and have less than 30 per cent calories from fat and no added trans fats. New and healthier meals for children are being developed that will replace fatty and sugary ingredients. The companies will use organic unsweetened apple sauce, low-fat milk and fresh apple slices.

8 These measures are seen as the fast food industry's contribution to minimising the risk of overweight children and young people. Unfortunately recent studies within the industry have frequently shown that some food and beverage companies do not abide by the rules they had agreed on.

(629 words)

Annotations

l. 14 *to boost sales:* to increase the number of items being sold; to make more profit
l. 20 *to yield returns:* to produce profit
l. 25 *merchandise:* things that people buy or sell
l. 33 *nutritious:* full of substances that a body needs to stay healthy or grow properly
l. 39 *to foster:* to encourage
l. 41 *to bear fruit:* to finally become effective (see German: "Früchte tragen")
ll. 45/46 *to commit (oneself):* to promise
l. 50 *trans fat:* mostly industrially created fat; unhealthy when consumed in big amounts
l. 57 *to abide by the rules:* to stick to/to follow the given laws/rules

Pre-reading activities

Task 1 When dealing with a new text you will usually find a lot of new, unknown words. It is a good idea to look up as many of those words as necessary in order to fully understand the text. Here is a list of some words that you might not know. Match the English words (A–J) with their German meanings (1–10).

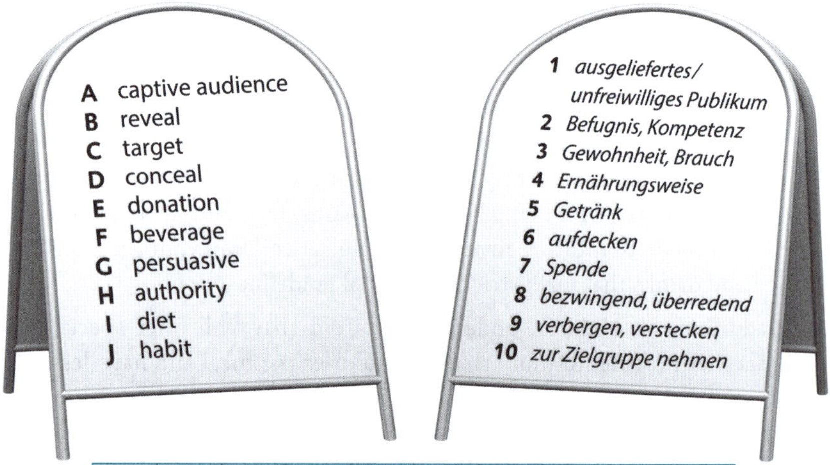

A	B	C	D	E	F	G	H	I	J
1									

Task 2 In the following text ("Do you hate adverts?") some words are incomplete. Reconstruct the original version by filling in the missing letters. The words may help you to understand the main text better.

Do you hate adverts?

All media, TV and the printed press, are heavily **dep** *e n d* **ent** on advertising revenue. Newspapers need money to **fin** ___ ___ ___**e** costs, which include paper, printing, distribution and, last but not least, salaries for editors, journalists, designers, cartoonists and photographers.

Publishers earn the necessary funds by selling space for ___ ___**verts** in the paper. Television channels cover costs by selling time for **com** ___ ___ ___ ___ ___**als** which are broadcast in **brea** ___ ___ during programmes. Many viewers are annoyed when the announcer interrupts the show with the phrase, "We'll be back after a short break! Stay tuned." To **av** ___ ___**d** viewers switching over to

another **c __ __ __nel**, many advertisers try to make their commercials entertaining.
However, thanks to the progress in computer and Internet **t __ __ __ __ __logy** another way of watching your favourite programmes has become available – and all of this independent of schedules set by the TV companies. Viewers can now __ __ __**ch** films and videos whenever they want. Streaming is the key word. Programmes are transmitted via **c __ __ __e** or over the Internet to users' tablets, laptops or TV sets. Taking advantage of people's aversion to adverts during programmes, new streaming platforms have been founded which do not **b __ __ __ __ __ast** commercials – at a cost, however. To enjoy advert-free television you have to subscribe to these streaming **ser __ __ __ __s**.

Understanding the text

Read the text and choose the correct box. **Task 3**

Tips

The purpose of a text
Ask yourself: Is the author trying to inform the reader about something? Does he want to give advice on a certain topic? Is he trying to warn the public by stating his opinion? He might even just want to entertain us with what he is writing.
You can check some elements to make sure that you understand the overall purpose:

- Have a look at the **general layout** of the text. Is it a newspaper article, an excerpt from a play or an advertisement? This may help you identify the correct type of the text.
- In the paragraphs of the text look for **signal words or phrases** that might show the intention of the author, e. g. "Recent studies show …" (informative), "In my opinion …" (argumentative), "Suddenly there was a bright light …" (narrative). In the given text you can also find a lot of facts and numbers that might help you with your answer.
- Look at the **headline** of the text and/or the **concluding paragraph**(s). Here you can often find the "**message**" of the author or sometimes a hint at the text's purpose.

The overall purpose of the author is to …

a) ☐ warn adults about the health dangers of fatty foods.
b) ☐ advise parents on how to limit media consumption of their children.
c) ☐ describe how social media have changed our society.
d) ☐ inform readers about how advertisers influence young children.

Task 4 Find the correct passage in the text.
In order to help you, the key words are underlined.
In which line(s) can you find information about the fact that …

- firms use advertising as a means of promoting public relations.
  (line(s): ______________)
- young children are unable to see through the tricks of the advertisers.
  (line(s): ______________)
- parents want their children to eat healthily.
  (line(s): ______________)
- fast-food restaurants will substitute fat and sugar with healthier substances.
  (line(s): ______________)
- food producers want to reduce the danger of young people becoming too fat.
  (line(s): ______________)

Task 5 Mark the appropriate definition with a cross (✗).

1. "product placement" (l. 24) means …
   a) ☐ displaying a product properly on the shelves in the supermarket.
   b) ☐ showing products in a film scene so that viewers see the brand name.
   c) ☐ stressing the importance of a product in adverts.

2. "persuasive intent of adverts" (l. 29) means …
   a) ☐ adverts want to make you buy a product.
   b) ☐ adverts emphasise the quality of a product.
   c) ☐ adverts inform you about a product.

3. "low-nutrition foods" (l. 35) means …
   a) ☐ food with little or no calories.
   b) ☐ food which keeps blood sugar levels down.
   c) ☐ food which is not very healthy (junk food).

Matura-style tasks

Read the text, then choose the correct heading (A–K) for each paragraph (0–8). There are two extra headings that you should not use. **Task 6**
The first one (0) has been done for you.

Tips

Matching
The following steps show you a possible way of dealing with this matching exercise:
- Read through the text before looking at the headings presented in the task.
- With a pencil write down a heading of your own choice (use your own words) next to each paragraph. You may also write a complete sentence summarising the paragraph.
- Read through the options and compare them with your own headings or notes.
- Be careful with the "distractors": they may give information that is not in the text.

A Adverts are everywhere
B Positive results of the new advertising code
C Healthier meals for the very young
D Media consumption of children and teenagers
E Some producers break the agreement
F Children watch too much TV
G The benefits of advertising
H The government's call for responsible advertising
I Companies need advertising to survive
J Parents see the dangers in the unhealthy food adverts
K The popularity of the web among the young and old

0	1	2	3	4	5	6	7	8
K								

Task 7 Part 1 – Find the information: Read the following statements (A–I) and compare them to the text. Find the corresponding passage or sentence in the text and highlight it with a marker.

A Children can be easily influenced by adverts.

B Firms invest large sums in adverts directed at young people.

C Advertisers sponsor theatre or opera productions.

D Normally, sponsoring a cultural event does not bring in a lot of money.

E Parents complain that advertisers create bad eating habits in children.

F The government takes action to ban harmful advertising.

G Producers are aware of the negative consequences of unhealthy foods.

H Fresh fruit is suitable for food processing.

I Some producers of food do not keep their promises.

Part 2 – Multiple Choice

Read the text again, then choose the correct answer (a, b, c or d) for assignments 1–5.
Put a cross (✗) in the correct box.
Use your work from Part 1 to find the correct options.

Tips

Exercises with multiple choice options are very common – especially in the "Matura".

- Read the assignments very carefully before reading the text for the first time. Usually they are in chronological order according to the information in the text.
- Look for key words and phrases in the text; but do not just fall for certain words – the context is even more important here.
- The wrong answers ("distractors") are there to set you on the wrong track; check and re-check your answers as thoroughly as possible.

1. Firms spend a lot of money on …
   a) ☐ TV adverts which tell parents what to buy for their children.
   b) ☐ adverts which entertain parents and children.
   c) ☐ commercials which fascinate younger and older audiences.
   d) ☐ commercials which are meant especially for young children.

2. The money with which firms sponsor theatre and opera productions …
   a) ☐ is a bad investment.
   b) ☐ pays off because it makes sales boost.
   c) ☐ is often not profitable.
   d) ☐ is now more necessary than ever.

3. The adverts which children watch on TV …
   a) ☐ give a totally wrong picture of family life.
   b) ☐ make children want to eat the wrong food.
   c) ☐ are completely different from their own experience.
   d) ☐ make kids ask their parents for more and more toys.

4. The aim of the new guidelines is to …
   a) ☐ make children eat the right kind of food.
   b) ☐ make the industry offer healthier food for kids.
   c) ☐ ban TV food adverts which are directed at children.
   d) ☐ tell parents what is good and healthy for their kids.

5. The new guidelines for healthier food for children …
   a) ☐ are not observed by all companies.
   b) ☐ must be improved by the authorities.
   c) ☐ have to be agreed on by more firms.
   d) ☐ have to be controlled by more studies.

Columbus – Adventurer across unknown seas

Text

When he died at the age of 54, he was ill and almost forgotten by his contemporaries. Today every child knows his name and what he achieved, but the man and his deed still provoke passionate debates. Christopher Columbus was born in Genoa, Italy, which at that time was an independent city-state and a busy port. He received little education – only much later as an adult did he learn to read and write – went to sea and started a career as a commercial agent. Having often heard reports of legendary westward voyages beyond Madeira and the Azores on his numerous journeys, Christopher Columbus studied old books and charts to acquire more information. He became convinced that Asia could be reached quickly by sailing west. According to his calculations Japan was about 4,800 km (3,000 miles) to the west of Portugal – a distance that could be sailed in existing ships. In 1484 the king of Portugal, John II, rejected Columbus' proposal to search for a route to Asia, but with his unyielding willpower Columbus eventually managed to win the support of the Spanish monarchs, Ferdinand V and Queen Isabella. On August 3, 1492, three small and simple ships set sail from Palos, Spain and landed on Guanahaní, an island in the Bahamas, on October 12. The expedition was met by Arawak, a friendly local population that Columbus called Indians, because he believed he had reached the East Indies. He renamed the island San Salvador ("Holy Saviour"), sailed on to Cuba and arrived back in Spain in March 1493. He was received enthusiastically, but over the years lost the support of the monarchs as he failed to find the gold they had hoped for and was replaced as governor general of all new lands in 1500.

What Columbus did not know on his departure from Spain was that the discovery he was to make would be more important and valuable than the route he failed to find. Columbus conducted his enterprise at a time when Europe was just awakening from the Dark Ages, leaving behind the belief that the earth was flat and stood at the centre of the planetary system and that man was the master of his own destiny. The voyage brought about a revolutionary change of perceiving the world and initiated an exchange between the New and Old Worlds of food, plants and animals, of inventions and cultural, religious and political concepts, which ultimately influenced the shaping of the societies on both sides of the Atlantic. What is known as the Columbian Exchange is also responsible for the transmission of infectious diseases, such as measles, which caused epidemics and led to the nearly complete destruction of the peoples of the newfound lands and their environment. The colonists abused the natives, exploiting them cruelly as slaves. They robbed them of their land, driving them away into the less fertile areas, decimating their population. It is therefore not surprising that not all people in the USA join in the celebrations on Columbus Day in October of each year. The fact that some see Columbus' arrival as a positive event, whereas others condemn it as the beginning of a genocide, proves the lingering impact of his accomplishment. Yet it would be just as unfair to hold Christopher Columbus responsible for the extinction of thousands of natives as to credit him alone for the expansion of the Old World. He should be seen as what he was: "The first European visitor to central America." Christopher Columbus died on May 20, 1506, still fighting for his rights, still believing that he had reached Asia. *(600 words)*

Annotations

l. 20 *proposal:* plan or suggestion to an official person or group
l. 48 *to exploit:* to use or abuse sb's workforce in an unfair way
l. 50 *to decimate:* to reduce in number; to destroy a large part of sth
l. 55 *extinction:* act of putting an end to sb or sth

Pre-reading activities

Task 8 Match the English words (A–L) with their corresponding definitions (1–12). In the following task you will need those words to complete a text.

A	awaken	1	undertaking or new project, esp. when bold/dangerous
B	belief	2	becoming awake, aware or active
C	deed	3	the act of ruining sth
D	destiny	4	the giving and taking of one thing for another
E	destruction	5	a passage by water or air to some place at some distance
F	discovery	6	to understand, to become aware of
G	enterprise	7	a strong opinion
H	exchange	8	an act, something done
I	numerous	9	refusing to accept or believe in sth
J	perceive	10	the act of finding out
K	reject	11	great in number or quantity
L	voyage	12	that which has happened or must happen to someone because of fate or luck

A	B	C	D	E	F	G	H	I	J	K	L
2											

Task 9 In the following text about Christopher Columbus some words are missing. Complete the text with the words from the list (A–L) of the task that you have just dealt with.

Tips

Have a close look at the context to find out which words work and which do not. Example: the article "an" in front of the third gap can only be followed by an adjective or a noun starting with a vowel.

October 12, 1492 marks the day of the arrival of Christopher Columbus on American shores after an almost endless ______ across unknown seas. The day of his landing was the end of a remarkable __________ and the beginning of an _________ of people and cultures between two different worlds. Columbus Day or Discovery Day has a special meaning in the United States and in _________ Latin American countries. Some see Columbus' _____ in a positive light, whereas others _______ this positive appreciation. Many Native Americans

__________ the arrival of the Europeans as a catastrophe, because Columbus' ____________ opened the door for the invasion of the North American continent by immigrants from the Old World. The influx of pioneers and settlers during the period of the westward movement changed the _________ of the indigenous population profoundly. There is a common _______ that the white man is responsible for the extinction of many tribes and the _______________ of Indian culture. Today Native Americans work for a process to re-________ old traditions by teaching the younger generation about their forefathers in special tribal schools and at universities.

Understanding the text

Task 10

The meaning of words:
Which of the given options is the best definition for the words (1–3)?
Choose the correct box. Feel free to use a dictionary if necessary.

1. "unyielding" (l. 20)
   - a) ☐ insufficient
   - b) ☐ unprepared
   - c) ☐ impatient
   - d) ☐ resolute
2. "revolutionary" (l. 41)
   - a) ☐ unknown
   - b) ☐ upsetting
   - c) ☐ unheard of
   - d) ☐ tragic
3. "lingering" (l. 54)
   - a) ☐ complete
   - b) ☐ unreasonable
   - c) ☐ lasting
   - d) ☐ final

Task 11

Scan the text for details to solve the following assignments.

1. Which of these countries is not mentioned in the text?

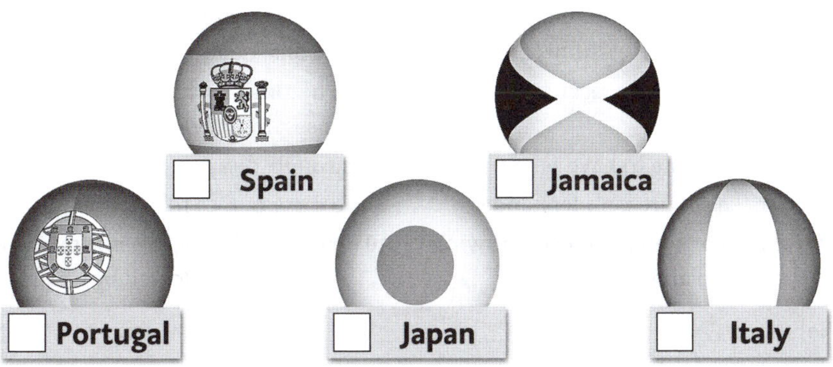

2. List the islands which are mentioned in the text.

____

____

3. Which adjectives describe the character of Columbus best?

a) ☐ uneducated b) ☐ studious c) ☐ greedy
d) ☐ daring e) ☐ incompetent f) ☐ wilful

Task 12 Fill the empty spaces with words from the main text, using the list with definitions below. The grey column gives you the name of the island where the first European colonies in the New World were established.

1	A													T			
					2	C					T						
						3	A				E						
									4	P							E
									5	A						E	
							6	C						N			
					7	C							E				
								8	C						T		
				9	F						E						
							10	M						S			

1 something which has been achieved or successfully completed

2 to ascribe something such as a personal quality to somebody

3 improper or incorrect use

4 to become aware of through the senses; to understand

5 to get or come to have as one's own

6 strongly disapprove of sth or sb

7 to make sb agree, understand sth

8 to carry out, to manage

9 (of land or soil) capable of growing crops or plants

10 mainly children's disease marked by red spots followed by a rash

Solution: ______________________

Matura-style tasks

Task 13

Read the following statements (a–h) and compare them to the text "Columbus – Adventurer across unknown seas". In the "Matura" you have to state if they are true or false and give the corresponding sentence from the text. In assignments b–d the first part (true or false) has been done for you. Find the correct sentence of the text and write down the first four words. In e–h you also have to decide if the statement is true or false. There is an example at the beginning (a).

Tips

When answering questions about whether a statement is **true or false**, you have to know the text well and you must be able to find the proof for an answer exactly in the text.

- Read the questions very carefully before reading the text. You can mark words/phrases that seem important in order to find them or synonyms within the text more easily.
- Be sure that you understand the statement completely. Think of possible ways of marking the question as false: e. g. "Columbus was the first and only discoverer of …" (g)
  → Was Columbus actually the first one?
  → Was he really the only one?
  → Did he actually discover the North (or maybe the South) American continent? …
- Look for synonyms or synonymous phrases for words in the text and the question.
- Make sure that you found the correct sentence and put down just the first four words!

Statement	True	False	First four words
a) Columbus based his voyage on the tales of other seafarers.	☒	☐	*Having often heard reports*
b) Columbus had no trust in the seaworthiness of the vessels of his time.	☐	☒	
c) Columbus was stripped of his post because he could not bring home enough gold.	☒	☐	
d) Finding a route to India was less significant than the discovery of America.	☒	☐	
e) When Columbus started his voyage most people in Europe believed that the earth was a sphere.	☐	☐	
f) Some people see Columbus' achievement in a very negative light.	☐	☐	
g) Columbus was the first and only discoverer of the North American continent.	☐	☐	
h) Columbus was always convinced he had found a new continent.	☐	☐	

Task 14 Read the text "Columbus – Adventurer across unknown seas" and answer the questions (a–h) using a maximum of four words. The first one (a) has been done for you.

Tips

Short-answer questions, where you have to put in a **maximum of four words**, are very common in the "Matura".

- Read the questions very carefully. The key words are underlined here to help you find the corresponding passage in the main text. (This will not be the case in the real "Matura"!)
- Mark the phrases/sentences in the text that give you the answer – even if it is more than four words; but make sure to put down not more than four words as your final answer.
- Usually there is not just one solution possible. Be confident with your answer. Even if it is not given exactly in the key, it might be credited as correct in the examination.

a) How did Columbus find out more information about voyages beyond the Azores?

studied maps and charts

b) What did Columbus try to find west of Portugal?

____

c) Where did Columbus think he had landed when he arrived on Guanahaní?

____

d) How long did Columbus' first voyage last?

____

e) What began between Europe and America after Columbus' discovery?

____

f) In which way was the health of the native population affected?

____

g) How did the Europeans treat the natives?

____

h) How did the Europeans destroy the livelihood of the Native Americans?

____

Working children

William is 11 and works in a cotton mill in the English Midlands. If you asked him how many hours he works each day, he probably couldn't tell you exactly. He usually works from 5 in the morning to 7 at night, but there are times when the factory owner keeps him working for as long as he wants him to. There are no clocks in thc mill, anyway. If William is late for work, he is punished, takes a beating, and has money deducted from his weekly pay. As he is small, his job is to dive in and out of the machinery picking up bits of stray cotton. Last month, William's friend James, two years younger and working in a coal mine, suffered a terrible accident. He was pushing a truck of coal along the narrow mine tunnel, when he suddenly stumbled and was run over by the heavy truck, losing his left arm. Not only has he suffered this bad injury, he has also been sacked from his job, and nobody pays for James' treatment. A catastrophe for his family as James was the only breadwinner.

Hamza is 10 and works in a small garment workshop producing children's clothes in a suburb in New Delhi. Sweat is pouring off his face as it is very hot and sticky and there is no ventilation in the factory. Hamza's job is to sew by hand tiny logos onto baby T-shirts during his 16-hour workday. He works here because his parents had to sell him to the factory owner in exchange for a loan so that they could keep their small piece of land, which belongs to the bank. Hamza does not know how long he will have to work to repay the loan. At the moment he does not earn any money, because he is still regarded as a beginner and learner. His friend Amitab, who is two years older and comes from the same village as Hamza, works in a quarry in Alwar, Rajasthan, loading heavy stones onto lorries.

William and James lived in the 19th century, and their working conditions began to improve when a number of Factory Acts were passed by the British Parliament to alleviate the worst exploitation of women and children working in factories and coal mines when the Industrial Revolution was in full swing. Labour reformers pressed for improvements and eventually, in 1847, a law which became known as the Ten Hours Act cut down working hours for women and children to effectively 10 hours a day.

Hamza and Amitab live today, in the 21st century. In Western industrialised countries there are strict laws protecting the health and safety of young people in the workplace. The legal working age is 13 or 15, depending on the difficulty of work. Part-time work for pocket money such as paper rounds or light agricultural jobs are allowed at an earlier age than full-time work – which in most countries is 16 or 18. Hamza and Amitab do not profit from these regulations because they live in a developing country. In emerging and developing economies the percentage of children who have to work is especially high. In many child sweatshops some children are only six.

Campaigners against child labour argue that globalisation is one of the roots of the problem of child labour in developing countries. To lower labour costs multinational corporations set up production plants in Asia where they employ children, who have to work long hours, often in unsafe or unhealthy conditions, barely earning a subsistence wage. The continued efforts of charity organisations like UNICEF and Global March seem to be bearing fruit. According to the ILO (the International Labour Organization) the global number of child labourers has declined since 2000, from 246 million to 168 million children. This progress has been achieved by stricter legislation and higher investments in education and social protection such as health care and security in old age. All in all, the fight against child labour is on the right track, but the goal of eliminating its worst forms has still to be met. *(683 words)*

Annotations

l. 12 *to sack:* to dismiss, to fire (from a job)
l. 13 *breadwinner:* a member of a family who earns money to support the others
l. 23 *quarry:* a large open area dug for mining stone
l. 38 *emerging:* rising, growing, up-and-coming
l. 45 *wage:* money that you earn for work

Pre-reading activities

Task 15

The following is a list of words from the main text with their German meaning. Unfortunately they have been jumbled up. Reconstruct the original versions. To start you off the first letter of the jumbled words is given.

Jumbled word	Solution	German
VILELETA	A L L E V I A T E	*erleichtern*
EUCDT	D _ _ _ _ _	*abziehen*
ORU	P _ _ _	*strömen*
LPNOXTTIIOΛ	E _ _ _ _ _ _ _ _ _ _ _	*Λusbeutung*
AETRNM	G _ _ _ _ _ _	*Bekleidung*
LLI	M _ _ _	*Fabrik; Mühle*
TRYA	S _ _ _ _	*verlorengegangen, heruntergefallen*
UCEINTEBSS	S _ _ _ _ _ _ _ _ _ _	*Existenz, Lebensunterhalt*
TWPESHOA	S _ _ _ _ _ _ _ _	*Ausbeutungsbetrieb*

Task 16

Complete the following text about slavery and bonded labour with the words in the stones. This will help you to understand the main text.

Although slavery is against the ____________ everywhere, it continues to exist in many parts of the world. Especially in Asian and African ____________ countries people of all ages are exploited as cheap ____________. The term 'slavery' is rarely used anymore. Instead, slavery is usually referred to as 'bonded labour' or 'human trafficking.' From the 17th to the 19th ____________

________ mainly British and Dutch ships made slave trading voyages between the continents of Europe, Africa and America. Because of the horrible conditions on the ships many black Africans died on the journey. In Louisiana and Mississippi the Africans worked in the hot and ______________ climate on the cotton fields of the white plantation ______________. The same tragedy happened on the other side of the world. South Pacific islanders were kidnapped from their ______________ and used as slaves on the ______________ and sugar cane plantations of Queensland, Australia. The brutal and shameful practice became known as 'blackbirding'. Today most bonded labourers work in agriculture, the service industry and in ________________. In the textile ________________ in some Asian countries even ______________ children are exposed to ________________ working conditions and can be fired – also called ________________ – from their jobs for no reason at all.

Understanding the text

Task 17 Reading for the gist:
Read the main text carefully and decide which of the alternatives provided is correct.

The text "Working children" is primarily about …

a) ☐ the misery of children during the Industrial Revolution.

b) ☐ working children in England, India and Australia.

c) ☐ the situation of working children in the past and the present.

d) ☐ the improvements in the situation of working children.

Tips

The technique of **reading for the gist** is important in order to understand the general meaning of a text. A common question is: "What is the text about?"
Try these methods and choose the one that suits you best:

- Read through the text two, three or even four times faster than you normally would.
- Read the headline and the first/last paragraph and look at pictures or graphics if there are any.
- Just read the first sentence of every paragraph.
- Do the quick reading first, then look at the suggested answers and re-read the text if necessary.

Scanning the text:

Task 18

Tips

If you are dealing with questions asking/looking for certain details, you have to **scan the text**. There is a broad variety of possible assignments for this kind of task. In the one that follows you need to extract information from the text to complete the grid. You can use these guidelines:

- Look at the grid to find out what kind of information you need: In this case you have to collect information about four people.
- Scan the text for names first. When you have found a name, look for a number (the person's age), a country or nationality, a job and a workplace that refer to this name. Do the same for the remaining persons.
- Mark the paragraphs concerning a certain person with one colour, the ones dealing with another person with a different colour, and so on.

Fill in the grid with the relevant information about the children mentioned in the text "Working children". Some items have already been filled in.

Name	Age	Country	Workplace	Job
			cotton mill	
James				
		India (New Delhi)		
	12			*load stones onto lorries*

Matura-style tasks

Task 19

Read the text "Working children". Find the sentence(s) in the text which can tell you something about a statement. Then decide whether the statements (a–g) are true or false and put a cross (✗) in the correct box. Write the first four words of the sentences found in the space provided. There may be more than one correct answer; write down only one. The first one (a) has been done for you.

Statement	True	False	First four words
a) There were no fixed working hours for William.	☒	☐	*He usually works from*
b) William operated a machine to weave cloth in the textile mill.	☐	☐	

c) Apart from James there was nobody in the family who earned any money.	☐	☐	
d) Hamza's employer bought the boy's family a small piece of land.	☐	☐	
e) Hamza and Amitab, who come from the same village and work in the same factory, are victims of exploitation.	☐	☐	
f) The worldwide exchange of goods today is partly responsible for the problem of child labour.	☐	☐	
g) Children in Asian factories often do not earn enough money to live on.	☐	☐	

Task 20 Read the text "Working children" (ll. 1–31). Answer the questions using a maximum of four words. Write your answers in the spaces provided. The first one (a) has been done for you.

Tips

- Read the questions very carefully and mark names and key words (see example a).
- Look for synonyms or synonymous phrases in the text; but be careful: If you find a corresponding word, it may be in a completely different context; for example: The first mentioning of "Hamza" and his work does not give you the answer to question c. You have to read on for the correct passage.

a) Why was William unaware of how long he worked every day?

no clocks in factory

b) Why was William especially useful for the job he had to do?

____

c) How did Hamza get into bonded labour?

____

d) Why was Amitab's job particularly harmful?

____

e) What effect did the Factory Acts have?

____

Read the text "Working children" (ll. 32–end). Add a <u>maximum of four words</u> to complete the sentences (a–d).
The first one (a) has been done for you.

Task 21

Tips

When you have to fill in words to complete a sentence, be sure to keep to the structure of the sentence; for example: In assignment a the first missing word can only be a noun phrase starting with an adjective or a noun.

a) Amitab and Hamza come from India, which still counts as a …

developing country .

b) Global companies often use children as workers because they want to …

______________________________.

c) Indications that the problem of child labour can be tackled successfully are, for example, …

______________________________.

d) One reason for the fact that the situation for children is improving is …

______________________________.

The secret of the mysterious crop field rings

Text

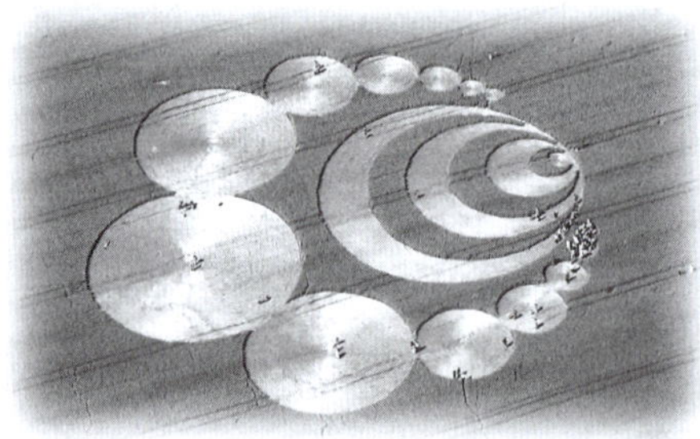

On a bright and sunny morning in 1981 farmer Timothy Jameson of Headbourne Worthy in Hampshire noticed something **(0)** ________. Overnight a very odd and huge circle had appeared in one of his wheat fields. The corn had been neatly flattened into a large circular pattern **(1)** ________.

Farmer Jameson did not see any footprints, so he couldn't explain how the circle had got there. He told the reporter of his local paper about his discovery – and it was soon reported nationwide. When in the following year more and more of these strange pictographs were sighted in southern England, research into the mystery began. Experts studied the beautiful geometric formations, speculating over their origin **(2)** ________. Some attributed the elaborate multi-circle designs to natural causes, such as cyclonic winds or bursts of energy, others saw them as the creations of hoaxers, and still others believed the circles were the work of intelligent beings from outer space. The "UFOlogists" were convinced that visitors from outer space were the creators because, in their view, the pictographs were much too precise to be manmade. The probe into the origin of the mysterious rings in the wheat fields continued. For many years **(3)** ________ the papers were full of reports of new sightings and explanations, more or less believable, of the supernatural phenomenon were published. To finally put an end to speculations two M.P.s called for the government to finance a serious scientific investigation **(4)** ________.

When two landscape painters David Chorley and Douglas Bower, both in their sixties, learned that the government had been asked to raise funds for an investigation, they felt it was time to reveal that they had contracted circles as a prank since 1978. As proof they allowed a reporter to watch them and take photographs. Moreover, the two men admitted that they had created as many as 25 to 30 new circles each growing season around southern England. After reading reports of flying-saucer sightings they had decided to flatten some corn to make it appear as if a UFO had landed. To their disappointment, nobody took any notice of their first circles until 1981, when the sighting by farmer Jameson was reported in the press and numerous articles and books appeared, maintaining the circle on **(5)** ______________ was the work of extra-terrestrials.

There is common agreement today that the circles, many of which display complex geometrical shapes, are the work of cunning artists. Under cover of darkness they create their pictographs anonymously in very short spans of time, carefully removing any human traces from the scene. Before they start their intricate work, many use computers, GPS equipment and lasers to help map out the ingenious patterns. In 1978 Bower had to create his straight lines using a circular wire attached to his cap. Even today hundreds of sophisticated crop circles still appear annually not only in southern England, **(6)** ___________. In spite of Bower's and Chorley's confessions in 1991 crop enthusiasts insist that the increasingly complex circles are not manmade, but owe their existence to alien collaboration. Every year, in great numbers, they hunt for new circles, reporting their sightings on the web, much to the frustration and anger of farmers, who do not want to have their fields invaded by crop circle enthusiasts, and cut down the formations and harvest the fields before the crowds arrive. In many cases only photographs of the original pictograph survive. *(555 words)*

Annotations

l. 16 *hoaxer:* sb who wants to make others believe sth that is not true
l. 28 *prank:* a trick which is played on sb to make him/her look silly; a joke
l. 38 *cunning:* very clever, crafty
l. 43 *sophisticated:* very well designed, very advanced and complex
l. 45 *confession:* a statement that you have done sth (wrong and perhaps illegal)
l. 50 *to harvest:* to gather/to bring in crops
l. 52 *to survive:* here: to remain

Pre-reading activities

Task 22 **Complete the text with the missing words, which are jumbled in the brackets in front of each gap. You can find the missing words in the main text. If you need some extra help, you can find the German translation right after the text.**

Many people like tales of **(r-y-y-s-e-m-t)** mystery **(1)** and horror. Fantastic creatures like monsters and mutants appear in hundreds and thousands of comics, video games and films, thus generating substantial **(s-u-f-d-n)** ______________ **(2)** for the entertainment industry. 19th century novelists created the characters of Frankenstein and Count Dracula, that are still very much alive and have made **(r-u-u-s-n-o-e-m)** ______________ **(3)** appearances in theatrical, film and television productions. Some weird creatures have even acquired cult status among **(t-n-t-e-h-s-a-i-s-u-s)** ______________ **(4)**, such as the "**(l-e-i-a-n)** ______________" **(5)**, an aggressive killer beast from the science fiction horror film series of the same name (1979–2012), whereas E.T. – short for **(x-a-e-l-r-t-t-e-r-t-r-e-i-a-s-r)** ______________ **(6)** – just wanted to call home (1984). Another favourite, Godzilla, the King of the Monsters, left its first **(c-e-a-s-r-t)** ______________ **(7)** on Earth in a Japanese film from 1954 and made spectacular returns to the big screen, for example in 1998 and 2014.

Reports of **(i-g-g-s-t-h-s-i-n)** ______________ **(8)** of unidentified flying objects (UFOs) make the headlines more or less regularly. As early as 1938 Orson Welles shocked the American public with his **(g-i-n-u-s-i-e-n-o)** ______________ **(9)** radio adaptation of H. G. Wells' novel *The War of the Worlds*. Panic broke out because listeners really believed that flying **(u-e-a-c-s-r-s)** ______________ **(10)** had landed on our planet. Four years earlier, in 1934, an English newspaper printed a photo of "Nessie", the Loch Ness monster. Many people do not only believe in its existence, they are also **(o-i-n-c-c-e-n-v-d)** ______________ **(11)** that the **(b-e-e-r-l-o-a-a-t)** ______________ **(12)** animal figures and geometrical designs in the Peruvian desert and in English **(e-h-a-w-t)** ______________ **(13)** fields are the works of an energy force from outer space. Be it as it may, the increasing amount of stories, novels, comics, videos and films featuring androids, replicants, monsters and mutants prove the popularity of people's belief in the unbelievable.

1	Geheimnis, Rätsel	**2**	Geldmittel
3	zahlreich	**4**	Fan, Liebhaber, Verehrer
5	Außerirdischer	**6**	außerirdisch, Außerirdischer
7	Spuren	**8**	Beobachtung, Sichtung
9	erfindungsreich, genial	**10**	Untertassen
11	überzeugt	**12**	sorgfältig ausgearbeitet, aufwändig
13	Weizen		

Understanding the text

Task 23

Reading for gist: Mark the most appropriate statement with a cross (✗).

What is the main text about?

a) ☐ The intensive scientific investigation of crop circles.

b) ☐ The first appearance of a crop circle in an English wheat field.

c) ☐ The different theories about the origin of crop circles.

d) ☐ How to make a crop circle.

Task 24

Reading for detail: Find the passages in the first paragraph of "The secret of the mysterious crop field rings" (ll. 1–24) which tell you that …
Write the first four words of the relevant passage in the table below.

Tips

Look for synonyms of the words in bold print.

Statement	First four words
a) … the straw was **carefully formed into a ring on the ground.**	*The corn had been*
b) … the discovery of the farmer **quickly made the headlines.**	
c) … some people thought **aliens had made the circles.**	
d) … the government was asked to **put up money for a proper examination.**	

Task 25 Read the list of events below (A–I) and re-establish the order in which they are presented in the text (0–6). Please note that there are <u>two</u> events which are not mentioned and you do not need.
As an example the first one (0) has been done for you.

Tips

- Read through A–I very carefully (maybe you can already establish a logical order).
- Read through the text very carefully while constantly checking whether one of the options has been mentioned.
- After having finished check your established order again.
- Be careful not to fall for the "distractors" (there are two of them).

A Different views about the origins of the circles
B Farmers are not at all pleased
C The general public loses interest in the phenomenon
D For several years the mystery is not solved
E How the first crop circles were made
F Farmer Jameson makes a discovery
G Crop circles appear all over the world
H Modern techniques used for the creation
I Time for a serious investigation has arrived

0	1	2	3	4	5	6
F						

Matura-style tasks

Task 26

Read the main text again. Parts of the text have been removed. Choose the correct part (A–I) for each gap in the main text (0–6). Write your answers in the spaces provided below. There are <u>two</u> extra parts that you should not use.
The first one (0) has been done for you.

Tips

For this **matching** exercise, you have to combine the skills that you have been testing out in the previous tasks:

- Read through the text carefully and check at every gap which of the given options is possible (maybe the chronological order can help you here).
- The sentence structure may also help you; certain options don't match with certain gaps. Pay extra attention to pronouns (who is the "he" in E and H) and conjunctions ("and", "but", "during") that have to be connected to a sentence in a different way from a relative clause (E), for example.
- After having finished check every paragraph with a gap to see if it still makes sense.

A and a general debate set in
B but around the world
C during summer months
D the traces of alien landings
E he had never seen before
F of about 30 metres in diameter
G of the rings in the wheat fields
H while he was fast asleep
I the field in Headbourne Worthy

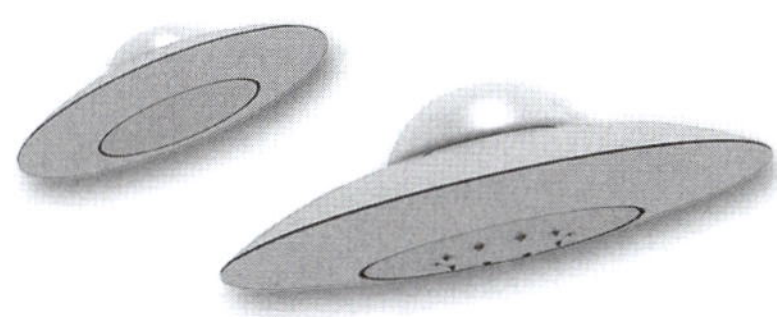

0	1	2	3	4	5	6
E						

Task 27 Read the text again, then choose the correct answer (a, b, c or d).
Put a cross (✗) in the correct box. The first one (0) has been done for you.

0. Farmer Jameson was surprised because …
   a) ☐ a huge spaceship had landed in his field.
   b) ☒ he saw a huge pattern in his field.
   c) ☐ his wheat field had been destroyed.
   d) ☐ the corn in his wheat field had been cut overnight.

1. Farmer Jameson had no idea how the pattern had got in his field because …
   a) ☐ he had slept solidly and had not heard anything.
   b) ☐ he had never seen such a design before.
   c) ☐ he could not detect any traces on the ground.
   d) ☐ of the enormous size of the design.

2. Scientists began to search for an explanation for the crop circles …
   a) ☐ after Farmer Jameson had told a reporter about his discovery.
   b) ☐ after the whole nation saw a report about it.
   c) ☐ after the discovery of numerous crop circles the following year.
   d) ☐ after an intervention from the government.

3. Some people believed the crop circles were …
   a) ☐ made by people as a joke.
   b) ☐ made by farmers to attract visitors.
   c) ☐ the work of touring visitors.
   d) ☐ designed by astronauts.

4. Eventually, two artists admitted that they had made the circles because …
   a) ☐ a journalist had discovered their secret.
   b) ☐ a reporter had published photographs showing the men in action.
   c) ☐ they didn't want the government to waste money on an investigation.
   d) ☐ they were no longer interested in contracting circles.

Cyber Crime

Text

The Internet is rapidly transforming the way we communicate, educate, and buy and sell goods and services **(0)** __________. As the web's potential to provide unparalleled benefits to society continues to expand, however, there has been an increasing recognition that the Internet can also serve as a powerful new medium for those who wish to commit unlawful acts. Every day **(1)** __________, criminals are invading countless homes and offices – not by breaking open windows and doors, but by gaining access into laptops, personal computers and wireless devices using hacks and malicious software.

To cover these offences a new word was coined: cyber crime or wire fraud. Cyber crime is the latest addition to the group called "white-collar crimes" and represents one of the greatest threats to a country's national security, economic prosperity and public safety. Some hackers take down vital systems, disrupting and sometimes disabling the work of hospitals, banks and emergency services. **(2)** __________ large amounts of money are needed to repair the systems hit by such attacks.

Communication over the Internet has now become easier than ever. With the rise **(3)** __________ of social network sites such as Facebook, Twitter, YouTube, Instagram and WhatsApp, people's ability to share photos and videos and exchange their personal thoughts and their political, religious and educational ideas with users all over the world **(4)** __________ is a simple click away. The negative side of the coin is that criminals breach social networks and steal the personal data of registered users. This unlawful activity is called identity theft. The personal data can then be used to order and pay for goods on the Internet. Therefore, warnings are issued to users of social network sites not to reveal too much personal data on their accounts. Social networking sites are not only misused for illicit activities such as theft, but also to cause fear in others **(5)** __________. As social networking is especially attractive and fascinating to young people who like to play games, have fun and keep in touch with friends, it can also become dangerous.

The office of the British Home Secretary has pointed to risks connected with the use of Facebook, Twitter and similar sites. They maintained that a child today could be at greater risk of abuse sitting in a bedroom on a computer than outside on the street. What they meant was that social networks are often used to be offensive or nasty towards other people. Cyber bullying or cyber abuse has become a widespread phenomenon and has caused concern among parents, **(6)** ___________. Repetitive and persistent personal attacks, insults and threats affect the victims of cyber bullying tremendously. There have been incidents of children thinking of hurting themselves because of bullying. Getting bullied on a social network is not only upsetting, it is also really hard to deal with. Anti-bullying experts offer help on how to reply to comments, remove tags, block and report someone to put a stop to the harassment. Criminologists agree that the rapidly increasing rate of cyber crime is a big problem and a challenge not only for private users, but also for governments and law enforcement agencies.

In view of the fact that the Internet is an important medium for commerce and communication both domestically and internationally, measures have to be adopted which ensure the safety and security of the web community. Home users are strongly advised to have an anti-virus programme installed on their computers or laptops **(7)** ___________. In the business world, most firms avail themselves of the services of specialists to improve cyber security. In the political arena, politicians work out laws and regulations in order to guarantee the continued growth and maturation of this medium and avoid the Internet turning into a haven for unlawful activity. *(612 words)*

Annotations

l. 7 *access:* ability to enter
l. 39 *repetitive:* sth that repeats itself again and again
l. 39 *persistent:* continuing, lasting
l. 44 *tag:* letter or symbol added to a text
l. 56 *haven:* a place of safety and shelter

Pre-reading activities

Task 28

The words from the box are missing from the text below. Match the correct letter (A–K) with the gaps (1–10) and find out about the different types of crime. The first one (0) has been done for you.

A: illicit • **B:** law enforcement agencies • **C:** homicide • **D:** avails • **E:** theft **F:** malicious • **G:** offence • **H:** offensive • **I:** fraud • **J:** elaborate • **K:** harassment

Breaking the law – The types of crime

Crossing a street when the lights are red is wrong because it is against a regulation, the Traffic Code, meaning it is against the law. Judges and lawyers call this type of breaking the law an **(0)** ____. However, a **(1)** ____ – which means breaking into a house or car or stealing from a shop – is much more serious and **(2)** ____. So is the use of violence, such as hitting somebody over the head or killing a person. These unlawful actions are not offences, they are considered violent crimes.

In addition, there is another type of crime, called white-collar crime. Unlike theft or **(3)** ____ this type of crime does not use violence. It **(4)** ____ itself of more refined, more **(5)** ____ methods. It cheats people and uses positions of trust and power in an unlawful way to gain money or property. A general term for these **(6)** ____ actions (activities against the law) is **(7)** ____. With the rise of modern technology another type of crime has come into existence: cyber crime, meaning crimes committed with the help of computers and the Internet. Bullying and **(8)** ____, which means attacking and insulting people in **(9)** ____ posts, have become a serious problem. For the police, the **(10)** ____, it is very hard to detect white-collar crimes.

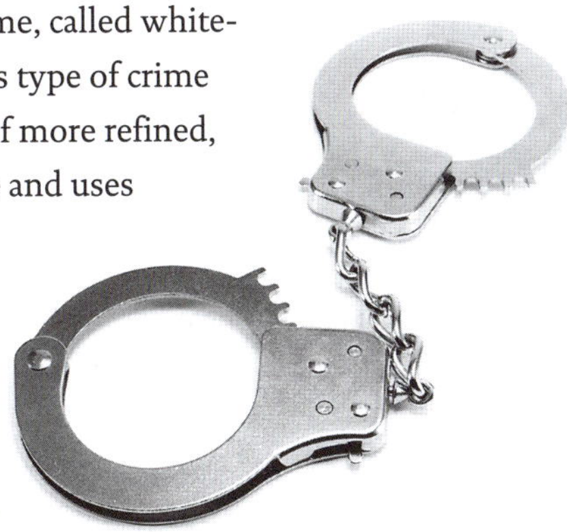

0	1	2	3	4	5	6	7	8	9	10
G										

Task 29 Use some of the words from the previous text to complete the puzzle. The definitions below will help you to find the correct position.
The first one (0) has been done for you.

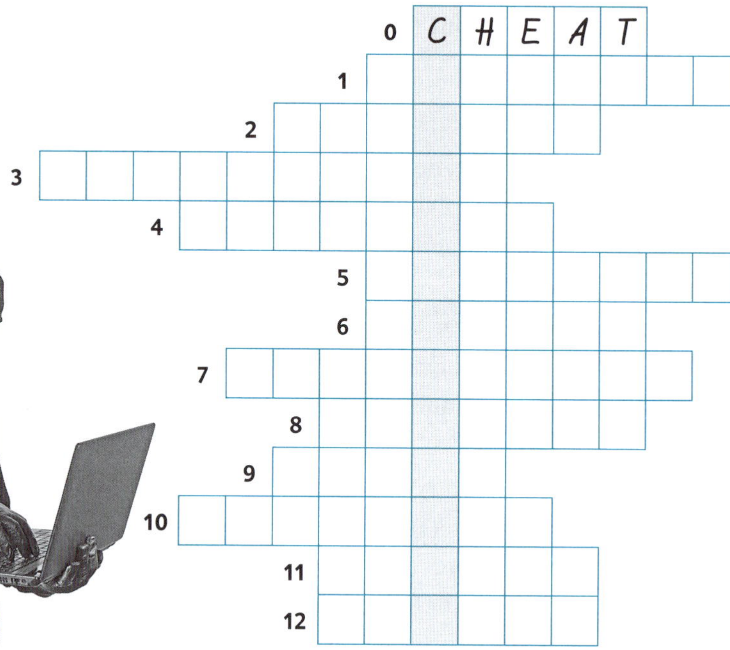

0 sth which is not honest

1 all of one's possessions

2 very clever, highly developed

3 illegal act committed on the Internet

4 pushing sb around causing pain and fear

5 not permitted, illegal

6 part of a shirt that goes around the neck

7 a rule or law

8 acting with great force or anger

9 a person whose job is to hear and decide matters in a court of law

10 taking something from sb without permission (ing-form)

11 speak to sb in a way that hurts him/her

12 find out, discover

Solution: ______________________

Understanding the text

Task 30

Read the following statements (a–e) and compare them to the text "Cyber Crime". Highlight the passages in the text where you can find the relevant information and write the first four words of the corresponding sentence in the table below. There is an example at the beginning (a).

Statement	First four words
a) People have become more aware of the dangers of the web.	*As the web's potential*
b) Staying in touch with people presents less difficulty today than in the past.	
c) Criminals purchase in online shops using names and addresses of unsuspecting users.	
d) Playing with the computer can be more dangerous than playing with other children.	
e) The Internet must not become a playground for criminals.	

Task 31

Sometimes English words have more than one meaning depending on the context they are used in, and often they cannot just be translated into one single German word. The following words should be familiar to you but be careful with their meaning.

1. Without looking at the text try to guess the meaning of the words. You can write down synonyms, an English description and/or German words that come to your mind.

   a) "maturation"

   meaning: ______________________________

   ____

   b) "challenge"

   meaning: ______________________________

   ____

   c) "transforming"

   meaning: ______________________________

   ____

2. Look at the word in the text and mark the exact meaning within the context with a cross (✗).

a) "maturation" (l. 55)
- ☐ development
- ☐ extension
- ☐ examination

b) "challenge" (l. 46)
- ☐ hard fight
- ☐ difficult task
- ☐ serious offence

c) "transforming" (l. 1)
- ☐ extending
- ☐ improving
- ☐ changing

d) "recognition" (l. 4)
- ☐ identification
- ☐ awareness
- ☐ gratitude

e) "disrupting" (l. 13)
- ☐ interrupting
- ☐ destroying
- ☐ altering

f) "avail (oneself)" (l. 53)
- ☐ pay for
- ☐ use
- ☐ rely on

Matura-style tasks

Task 32 Read the text "Cyber Crime". Some parts are missing. Choose the correct part (A–J) for each gap (1–7). There are two extra parts that you should not use. The first one (0) has been done for you.

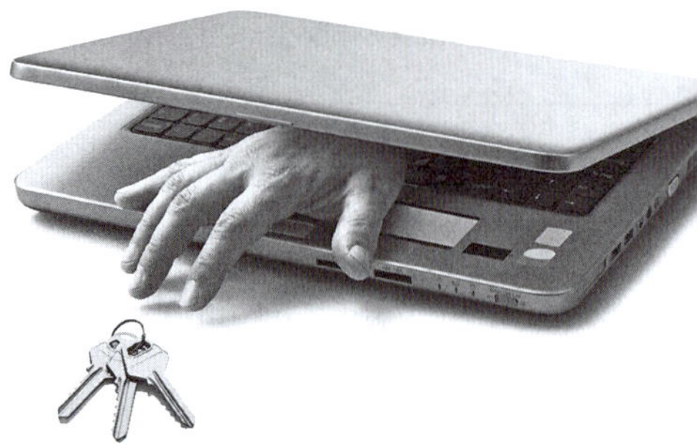

A nationally and worldwide
B are increasing dramatically
C educators and politicians
D and around the clock
E through threats and intimidation
F it is estimated that
G in real time
H and the increasing usage
I the continued efforts of the government
J to provide protection against Internet fraud

0	1	2	3	4	5	6	7
A							

Task 33

Read the complete text about cyber crime. (You can find it in the key to Task 32). First decide whether the statements (a–i) are true or false and put a cross (✗) in the correct box. Then identify the sentence in the text which supports your decision. Write the first four words of this sentence in the space provided. The first one (a) has been done for you.

Statement	True	False	First four words
a) The Internet constantly offers new possibilities.	☒	☐	*As the web's potential*
b) Unfortunately, criminals take advantage of the enormous capabilities of the web.	☐	☐	
c) Crimes on the web have been committed for a long time.	☐	☐	
d) There are people who breach networks and destroy data.	☐	☐	
e) Users are advised not to publish too many details about themselves and their families on the Net.	☐	☐	
f) Teachers worry about the increasing number of threatening and intimidating messages.	☐	☐	
g) Specialists can help effectively to stop people being abused.	☐	☐	
h) Official institutions and the police are more affected by cyber crime than private individuals.	☐	☐	
i) Even computer programmes that detect malicious software cannot help much.	☐	☐	

Obesity – a major health concern

Text

Sharmeli, 16, and her friend Charmaine, 14, loved the supersized meals of their favourite fast food restaurant. A muffin in the morning and the Double Burger meal with an apple pie in the evening plus several soft soda drinks were their staple diet. Their family doctor diagnosed both of them as obese, because their body mass index was much too high. The BMI, which assesses weight relative to height, for people of normal weight ranges between 18.5 and 25. Anybody with a BMI of 30 or higher is regarded as obese. Sharmeli, who is 1.6 metres tall and weighs 122 kilogrammes, had a BMI of 47.7, while Charmaine's was 35.5. The parents of the teenagers took the fast food restaurant to court, arguing that it was responsible for their children's being overweight because it did not provide the necessary information about the health risks associated with its meals.

Obesity has become a global epidemic which affects people of all ages and incomes. The number of overweight and obese people in the world has surged in the past three decades to more than 2 billion – nearly 30 per cent of the population of the planet. The problem is particularly urgent in the richer countries. In the United States and the United Kingdom 70 per cent of adults are either overweight or obese. However, excess weight is no longer a problem of the rich Western countries alone. Although in many low- and middle-income countries people suffer from hunger or starvation, overweight and obesity have become a health concern in a number of emerging economies. Since international fast food chains opened up branches in China and India, the percentage of people who are too fat has risen to 20 and 11 respectively. The problem also affects the Middle East and North Africa, where more than 60 per cent of adults are overweight or obese.

Childhood obesity has become the No. 1 health concern among doctors, educators and parents, topping drug abuse and smoking, because it has been proved that a healthy diet in childhood plays an essential role in growth and development, educational performance and avoidance of chronic disease throughout life. There are also psychological effects: Obese children are more prone to low self-esteem, negative body image and depression.

For a long time physical inactivity has been regarded as the major reason for the increasing number of fat people. However, in view of the fact that more people practise some sort of sport today than ever before, the search for the real causes were intensified. Recent studies prove that the main culprit is the excessive intake of sugary and fatty foods. People in general, and children in particular, eat too many sweets and snacks in-between meals and drink too many sugary drinks. All of these harmful foodstuffs are particularly heavily promoted by the food industry and are easily accessible everywhere – for example at sweet stalls or vending machines. As a result, the imbalance between energy input (calories obtained from food) and energy output (calories expended in the basal metabolic rate and physical activity) is responsible for people putting on weight. Overweight causes a lot of dangerous illnesses, such as heart failure, diabetes and cancer, and reduces people's life expectancy.

In order to avoid overweight and diet-related chronic diseases, nutritionists recommend a healthy diet which should comprise carbohydrates, fats, proteins, minerals and vitamins – all in moderation. This means you should eat a small amount of bread, cereals, potatoes and other starchy foods, plus meat, dairy products, fish or pulses, fruits and vegetables, and only low amounts of fat, sugar or salty foods. Any one-sided diet causes more harm than good. People are encouraged to eat at least five or, even better, seven portions of fresh fruit and vegetables a day, because this ensures an adequate supply of micronutrients like vitamins.

In conclusion, it has become more urgent than ever to combat overweight and obesity and educate children – and adults alike – about a nutritious diet and encourage them to take responsibility for their health and weight. It was no surprise that the lawsuit of Sharmeli and Charmaine, the obese teenagers, was eventually dismissed because the judge told the girls that they themselves were responsible for their overweight. Common sense should have told them that eating so many fatty meals was not conducive to their health.

(720 words)

Annotations

l. 8 *to assess:* to set the value of
l. 36 *prone to:* likely to suffer from
l. 40 *culprit:* person or fact responsible for damage/harm
l. 47 *basal metabolic rate:* the minimum number of calories your body burns
l. 54 *pulse:* edible seed of a plant (e. g. pea, lentil, bean)
l. 62 *lawsuit:* a case brought before a court of law

Pre-reading activities

Task 34 The following words are synonyms for words that are necessary to understand the text. Use the jumbled words to find those words in the word search puzzle below. The first one has been done for you.

Synonym	Jumbled word
advocate/approve	MEORCMDEN
corpulence/being too heavy	VEOREIHWGT
cut down	EERUDC
dangerous	RMHAULF
hunger	TISOATVNRA
illness	SEASIDE
long-lasting	HCNICRO
nourishing	UTNTIRIUSO
plant	EVETAEBGL
support/advance	POTEROM

Y	B	W	F	A	O	V	E	R	W	E	I	G	H	T	X	U
E	K	X	F	T	S	T	H	W	A	C	W	R	K	N	B	P
Y	Q	W	U	R	P	R	O	M	O	T	E	V	S	D	S	E
H	L	S	F	V	Z	V	M	G	Z	W	G	U	P	I	T	R
G	I	Q	Q	O	J	S	D	Z	T	D	O	J	D	S	A	K
I	X	S	N	B	Q	W	J	L	Y	I	E	L	L	E	R	O
V	R	O	A	G	S	F	F	O	T	G	G	U	W	A	V	E
E	X	A	I	J	E	K	T	I	S	K	F	S	U	S	A	H
G	X	J	Z	H	C	V	R	B	B	M	O	Y	W	E	T	N
E	E	Z	C	U	M	T	Q	I	R	T	Y	S	J	E	I	D
T	F	X	L	B	U	F	A	A	Y	A	K	W	C	V	O	E
A	G	O	Q	N	E	W	H	I	W	K	J	U	Z	K	N	P
B	N	B	X	A	A	R	I	X	R	H	D	M	R	J	T	J
L	C	B	X	Y	S	O	M	K	R	E	E	L	R	B	P	R
E	Z	C	H	R	O	N	I	C	R	C	N	S	V	B	J	D
R	E	C	O	M	M	E	N	D	R	J	B	T	Q	D	Z	G
Y	K	P	V	I	E	X	H	K	W	I	F	O	X	E	S	B

Finish off the crossword puzzle.

Task 35

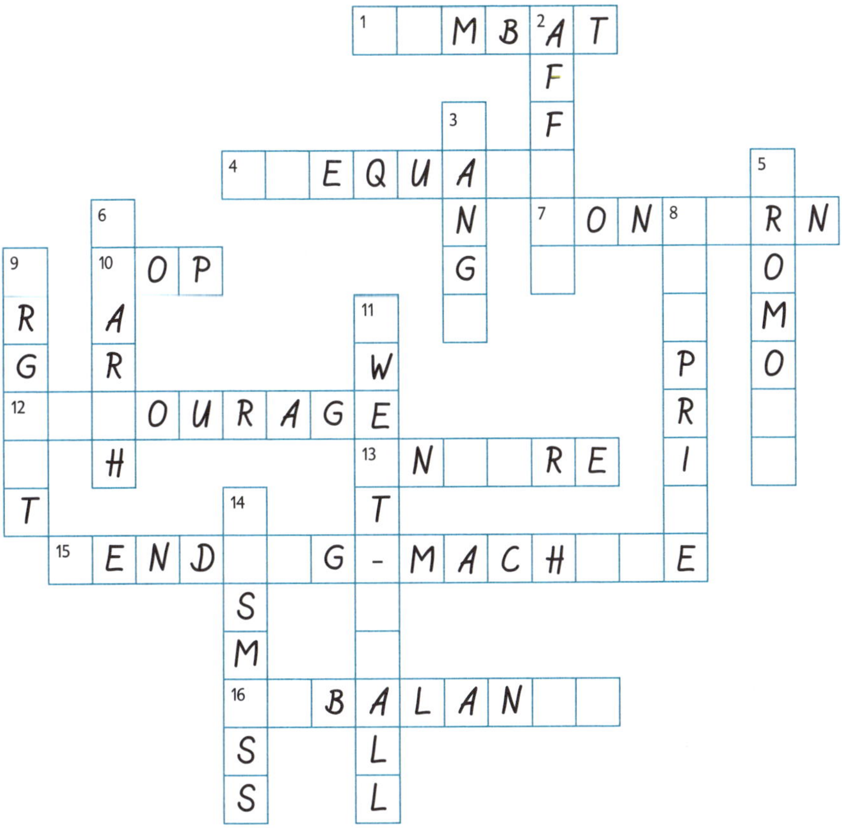

Across

1 fight against sth bad
4 good enough in quality and quantity
7 feeling of worry
10 be higher than
12 give hope or support
13 make sure or certain that sth will be the case
15 mechanical apparatus for the sale of cigarettes, sweets, drinks etc.
16 disturbed relation between two things

Down

2 have an influence on
3 vary or extend between two limits
5 advertise to increase sales
6 white substance in many foods, esp. in cereals, potatoes
8 be made of; have as parts
9 needing immediate action
11 a stand for the sale of confectionery made with sugar
14 refuse further hearing of a law case

Task 36 The following chart shows the assessment of the Body Mass Index (BMI) for a typical/exemplary 19-year-old male person (height: 180 cm).
Put the missing categories "obese", "overweight" and "normal" in their correct positions in the chart.

Category	Weight (in kg)	BMI
underweight	less than 57 kg	below 18.5
	57–81 kg	18.5–24.9
	82–99 kg	25–29.9
	more than 99 kg	30 or higher

Understanding the text

Task 37 Reading for the gist: Read the text "Obesity – a major health concern" and mark the best answers with a cross (✗).

1. The text is mainly about obesity …
   a) ☐ in developing countries.
   b) ☐ in the USA and the UK.
   c) ☐ as a global problem.

2. According to the text the number of obese people …
   a) ☐ has always been high in poorer countries.
   b) ☐ is declining in industrialised countries.
   c) ☐ is especially worrying in richer countries.

3. The author gives advice on …
   a) ☐ how to avoid obesity.
   b) ☐ how to take fast food chains to court.
   c) ☐ how to tackle the problem in emerging countries.

Task 38

Read the text "Obesity – a major health concern" and fill in the grid with the relevant information. To give you an example the data of one country have been filled in.

Country	Percentage of overweight or obese people
USA	*70 % (seventy per cent)*

Task 39

Look for the text passages which fit the German translations below and write down the correct lines in the table. The first example (a) has been done for you.

Statement	Line(s)
a) … Erfrischungsgetränke gehörten zu ihrer Grundnahrung	*ll. 5/6*
b) … verklagten das Schnell-Imbiss-Restaurant	
c) … ist in den letzten drei Jahrzehnten plötzlich angestiegen	
d) … ein Gesundheitsproblem in einigen Schwellenländern	
e) … sind eher anfällig für schwaches Selbstwertgefühl	
f) … war ihrer Gesundheit nicht zuträglich	

Matura-style tasks

Task 40 Read the text about "Obesity – a major health concern." Answer the questions (a–f) using a maximum of four words. The first one (a) has been done for you.

a) Why were the girls diagnosed as obese?

BMI was too high

b) When are people regarded as obese?

____

c) What made obesity levels rocket in China and India?

____

d) How did doctors traditionally explain people's overweight?

____

e) Why is the traditional explanation no longer valid?

____

f) Why is eating several portions of fresh fruit and vegetables every day especially healthy?

____

Task 41 Read the text "Obesity – a major health concern", then choose the correct answer (a, b, c or d) for assignments 1–5. Put a cross (✗) in the correct box. The first one (0) has been done for you.

0. Two teenagers' parents sued a fast food restaurant because …
   - a) ☐ the BMI of their children was too high.
   - b) ☒ they held the restaurant responsible for their daughters' overweight.
   - c) ☐ they wanted compensation for health costs.
   - d) ☐ they were no longer served their favourite meals.

1. Obesity is an urgent problem …
   a) ☐ in South Africa and the Middle East.
   b) ☐ concerning mainly adults.
   c) ☐ concerning the younger generation.
   d) ☐ for young and old, rich and poor alike.

2. Obesity in younger children …
   a) ☐ has similar effects to smoking.
   b) ☐ leads to social isolation.
   c) ☐ has become more worrying than drug abuse.
   d) ☐ cannot be avoided today.

3. People put on too much weight because …
   a) ☐ they sit around instead of moving.
   b) ☐ they give in to the promises of advertising.
   c) ☐ food has become more sugary.
   d) ☐ they eat more than their body needs.

4. Nutritionists recommend that …
   a) ☐ people eat mainly vegetables and leave out fat.
   b) ☐ meals consist of mainly starchy foods.
   c) ☐ people eat all sorts of food, but not in large quantities.
   d) ☐ people eat small meals five or seven times a day.

5. The complaint of the parents of the two girls was unsuccessful because …
   a) ☐ the judge did not believe their claims.
   b) ☐ the restaurant presented evidence against the girls.
   c) ☐ the judge ruled that the girls themselves were responsible.
   d) ☐ the judge did not regard fast food as harmful.

Allgemeine Hinweise

Viele Schüler empfinden den Hörverstehensteil von Englischklausuren als besonders schwer und anspruchsvoll und haben davor offenbar den meisten Respekt. Der Bereich „**listening comprehension**" gilt als schwierig, da man sich auf verschiedene Sprecher einstellen muss und in einer begrenzten Anzahl von Hördurchgängen alle Informationen aus dem Gehörten herausfiltern soll. Das Ungewisse und die starre Abfolge der Aufgaben schrecken viele. Dabei kann man sich auf diesen Prüfungsteil sehr gut vorbereiten – und dieser Band soll Sie dabei zielgerichtet unterstützen.

Aufbau des Hörverstehens in der Zentralmatura

Der Bereich Hören besteht in der zentral gestellten Englisch-Matura aus **vier verschiedenen Hörtexten**, zu denen **unterschiedliche Aufgaben** gestellt werden, die alle im Folgenden erläutert und trainiert werden sollen. Die englischen Audioaufnahmen werden in der Reife- und Diplomprüfung immer zweimal aufeinander folgend abgespielt, wobei vor, zwischen und nach dem Anhören eine kleine Zeitspanne gegeben wird, in der die jeweilige Aufgabe reflektiert und natürlich beantwortet werden soll.

Diese Vorgehensweise können Sie mit der beigelegten **MP3-CD** sehr gut nachstellen oder sich die Hörtexte öfter und genauer anhören. Zu Beginn der Vorbereitungsphase können Sie die Texte ruhig beliebig oft abspielen – je näher die Matura aber rückt, desto mehr sollten Sie unter Prüfungsbedingungen üben und desto weniger Hördurchgänge sollten Sie benötigen.

Aufbau der „Topics"

Die Themen der Hörtexte bzw. Aufgaben der Matura sind breit gefächert, darum wurde auch in diesem Trainingsband auf Abwechslung bei den Themen Wert gelegt. Das Kapitel „listening comprehension" ist – wie auch das Kapitel „reading comprehension" – **thematisch** (nach „Topics") **strukturiert**. In den hier vorliegenden „Topics" werden Sie **schrittweise** in die verschiedenen Aufgabentypen der Matura **eingeführt** und auf den Hörverstehensteil der englischen Reifeprüfung gezielt vorbereitet. Gleichzeitig können Sie an einer breiten Auswahl an Themen diese Aufgabenarten trainieren, die sowohl für Maturanten der AHS als auch der BHS geeignet sind.

Bevor Sie mit den „Topics“ loslegen, sollten Sie aber noch die hilfreichen Strategien und Arbeitstechniken sowie die Vorstellung der Aufgabentypen in den folgenden Abschnitten eingehend studieren.

Die einzelnen „Topics“ sind wie folgt aufgebaut:

- **„Pre-listening activities“** geben einen Einblick in die Thematik des Hörtextes und helfen Ihnen dabei, unbekannte Wörter vor dem ersten Hören zu verinnerlichen. Jedes „Topic“ enthält zwei dieser vorbereitenden Aufgaben.
- **„While listening – Getting to know the text“:** Diese Aufgaben stellen eine Möglichkeit dar, sich in den Text „einzuhören“ und sich einem Hörtext und der folgenden Bearbeitung in den Matura-Aufgaben in Teilschritten zu nähern; sie zeigen Ihnen auch Strategien, die Sie bei typischen Matura-Aufgaben anwenden können.
- **„While listening – Matura-style task“:** Hier wird eine mögliche Prüfungsaufgabe dargeboten. Der Umfang und die Schwierigkeit orientieren sich an den Musteraufgaben, die vom „BIFIE“ freigegeben wurden. Die Verteilung dieser „Tasks“ auf die „Topics“ sehen Sie in der Tabelle auf Seite 58.

Lösungsteil

Die Lösungen zu den Aufgaben sowie die Transkripte zu den Hörtexten finden Sie im **„Key“** am Ende des Buches. Hier erhalten Sie auch zusätzliche Hinweise zur Beantwortung und etwaige Erläuterungen zu Lösungswegen. Sie können nach jeder gemachten Aufgabe die Lösung nachschlagen oder erst am Ende eines „Topics“ ihre Ergebnisse überprüfen – das bleibt Ihnen natürlich frei gestellt. Vom transkribierten Hörtext sollten Sie jedoch erst Gebrauch machen, wenn Sie etwas nach mehrmaligem Hören nicht verstehen können oder eine gemachte Aufgabe noch einmal überprüfen wollen. Es bietet sich gerade am Anfang der Prüfungsvorbereitung an, beim Überprüfen der Lösungen die Höraufnahme noch einmal abzuspielen.

„Tips“-Kästen

Tips

In diesen Kästen finden Sie **Hinweise** speziell **zu den jeweiligen Aufgaben:**

- Sie sollen Ihnen **Strategien** vermitteln, wie Sie diese und auch ähnliche Aufgaben bearbeiten können.
- Aufgabenformen, die für die Matura besonders relevant sind, werden hier, sollten sie zum ersten Mal im Kapitel vorkommen, **Schritt für Schritt erläutert.**

Reihenfolge der „Topics“

Der **Schwierigkeitsgrad erhöht sich** von „Topic“ zu „Topic“, sodass Sie sich allmählich steigern und dem Niveau der Reifeprüfung „step-by-step“ nähern können. Wir empfehlen daher, die Aufgaben in der vorliegenden Reihenfolge zu bearbeiten.

MP3-CD

Die **Audiotracks** der beiliegenden MP3-CD sind jeweils neben den Aufgaben angegeben. Sie können den Schwierigkeitsgrad selbst steuern, indem Sie während der Aufnahme pausieren oder einen Track mehrmals wiederholen. Die Audiotracks zu den „Matura-style tasks“ können Sie selbst so abspielen, wie es in der Matura getan wird; befolgen Sie hierzu die Anweisungen zur Anzahl der Hördurchgänge und zu den Pausen in den Arbeitsaufträgen. Zu Übungszwecken können Sie ruhig längere Pausen machen oder die Tracks häufiger anhören. Sie werden merken, wenn Sie erst etwas Routine bei der Bearbeitung solcher Aufgaben haben, fällt es auch nicht mehr schwer, sie unter „Matura-Bedingungen“ zu lösen.

... and now let's switch to English to get you ready for your final exams.

Useful techniques and strategies in listening tasks

Before the first listening

The first thing you should always do when confronted with a task is to **read through the instructions very carefully** so that you know exactly what to do. In the "Matura" you will be given 45 seconds before the listening starts, so you should prepare for that by practising as much as possible within this time frame. If you are a quick reader, you can even use a pencil or marker to highlight words that you think may be important or may show up in the audio text.

During the first listening

During the first listening always remember that the questions or exercises are presented in **chronological order** – meaning that if you have just heard information that relates to a question, you should not think about it for too long but move on to the next one. You will always have time between the two listenings and, of course, after the second listening to check your answers again. However, try to **do as many assignments as possible** during the first listening and mark the ones you are not sure about so that you can check them before or during the second listening.

Between the first and second listening

After the first listening, you should **check your answers**. Did you fill in every gap? Can you spot any "distractors" (i. e. wrong options that are there to distract you from the correct one)? Is there anything you did not hear or understand at all? Prepare yourself for the final listening – you could highlight the questions that you did not answer during the first listening.

During and after the second listening

During the second listening you have to do two things: you have to **check answers** that you are not sure about and **fill in the missing ones**. Make sure that you do not get sidetracked by thinking about answers already given during the first listening. This will cost you a lot of precious time and pupils tend to alter answers that are already correct. Be confident about your decisions and move on!

Finally, you will have time to check your answers once again after the second listening.

Don't panic

In most cases you will not be able to understand every word or phrase and sometimes background noises or exotic accents and possibly very fast and unclear speakers make it hard to get everything within a recording. Do not panic or get frustrated! Focus on your task. Most of the time you do not need every single word or sentence in order to complete it.

Transcript

Make use of the transcription of the listening text, which you can find in the key section of the book, only if you really cannot understand something in the text and after you have attempted all the tasks in a topic. It is an additional tool which, of course, will not be available to you in the "Matura".

Common listening comprehension tasks of the "Matura"

Short-answer questions / Gap filling

Gaps are usually filled with a maximum of four words. The words may come from the text or they may be an interpretation of what you hear in the recording. When filling in the gaps, keep as close as possible to the meaning of the text and check your solution during the second listening if you can.

There are different ways this kind of task may be presented. The most common ones are:

- there are questions and you have to answer them in no more than four words,
- you are given beginnings of sentences and you have to finish them in no more than four words or
- there are gaps within sentences which you have to fill in with no more than four words.

Example

Listening text:
"Increasingly new media technology allows people an inside view of how the White House operates."

Task: Fill in the gaps.

Technology has given the American public the opportunity to ______________ ____________________ the White House and discover how it operates.

Answer:
look inside / see inside

Tip: If you cannot fill the gap in no more than four words, write the answer in pencil or on a piece of paper, then once the recording stops rewrite it, keeping within the required number of words. Consider using short forms; they count as one word, not two.

Matching

In this kind of task you usually have to …

- **match beginnings of sentences to their endings or**
- **match given answers to questions about the text.**

Read through the options and do not forget that some of them must not be used. They try to "distract" you from the correct options – therefore they are called "distractors". Listen carefully to match the correct parts.

Example

Listening text:
"So I decided to change our diet and […] it was really simple things; […] I saw some really immediate results with just those minor changes. And I thought, well, if I could help other families […] in my role as First Lady, that would be a good thing." (Topic 9)

Task: Match the beginning of each sentence to the correct ending.

A She only changed …
B Helping others is …
[…]

1 something she should do as the President's wife.
2 a lot of results that you can see.
3 little things in their diet.
[…]

Answer:

A	B	…
3	1	…

Tip: You should always check if you can rule out answer options that seem unlikely because they clearly do not logically fit. Do so before listening to the text and focus on the remaining options.

Multiple Choice

In a listening task with multiple choice options you have to listen very carefully to the context in the recording. Usually the "distractors" present words or phrases that you can hear in the recording but are given in a wrong or even opposite meaning or context. Therefore, you also have to read the statements thoroughly before or between the listening phases.

Example

Listening text:

"JOHN VIDAL: Since you wrote your book 40 years ago, population has increased almost as much as you predicted." (Topic 8)

Task/Answer:

Paul Ehrlich's book is …

a) ☐ correct in every word.

b) ☐ a real bestseller.

c) ☒ 40 years old now.

d) ☐ predicted to be true.

Tip: Always look at the other options to make sure that you have really found the correct one. Check your answers during the second listening.

Where to find the different "Matura-style" tasks

In the table below you can see in which topic you will find the different types of "Matura tasks":

Matura-style tasks	Topics					
	7	8	9	10	11	12
Multiple Choice	✗			✗	✗	
Matching		✗		✗		✗
Gap filling/Short-answer questions			✗		✗	✗

Life in the UK – Citizenship Test

Pre-listening

Task 42

Think about what the topic "Citizenship Test" will concern and write down your thoughts.

____

____

____

____

____

Task 43

What do you think the questions in the citizenship test will be about? Choose all the topics that you would expect to find in it.

While listening – Getting to know the text

Task 44 (T 1)

Now listen to the text and decide what the purpose of it is. Mark the best statement in your opinion with a cross (✗).

The purpose of the text is to …

a) ☐ show how people from other countries live in the UK.

b) ☐ inform people that employers now require them to take the test.

c) ☐ promote interest in the test and encourage foreigners to take it.

d) ☐ explain that the test is necessary for foreigners wishing to live in the UK.

Task 45 (T 1)

Listen to the text and connect the pictures of the speakers to their names and to the statements about them. Listen to the recording again if you don't get all the answers. Two lines have already been drawn for you.

Jevin

Salem

Thea

… is from South Africa.

… advises reading the questions carefully.

… passed the test.

… is married to a British citizen.

… hasn't taken the test yet.

While listening – Matura-style task

Task 46

T1

Study the task carefully for 45 seconds, then listen to the recording twice. While listening, mark the correct answer (a, b, c or d) with a cross (✗). After the second listening you have 45 seconds to check your answers. The first one (0) has been done for you.

Tips

Multiple Choice

- Read the assignments and all possible options very carefully before the first listening.
- Highlight words that seem important in order to find them more easily during the listening; for example in the first assignment (0) concentrate on listening to what "Salem" says about her being "motivated".
- If you are not sure which ending is correct, circle the letter (with a pencil) that you might choose and check it during the second listening.
- After the second listening you should mark your final answers with a cross (✗).
- If you need to do so, you can listen to the recording a third time, of course, as this is not the "Matura" … – not yet!

0. Salem's decision was motivated by …
   a) ☐ moving to the UK.
   b) ☐ getting married.
   c) ☒ other people taking the test.
   d) ☐ knowing the test was easy.

1. The main advice is to …
   a) ☐ find a quiet place to study.
   b) ☐ find out a lot of facts for yourself.
   c) ☐ go to a qualified person for lessons.
   d) ☐ use the government's material.

2. One recommendation is to …
   a) ☐ begin with familiar areas to bring success.
   b) ☐ learn the facts and figures initially.
   c) ☐ take shortcuts whenever possible.
   d) ☐ ask friends to help you learn.

3. Thea probably failed the test initially because she …
   a) ☐ was not well prepared. b) ☐ wasn't really focused.
   c) ☐ did it too quickly. d) ☐ didn't have 25 minutes.

4. People don't always have to …
   a) ☐ take the test to become a British citizen.
   b) ☐ study at home.
   c) ☐ take the online test first.
   d) ☐ practise the questions every day.

5. People aiming for citizenship need …
   a) ☐ the ability to read and write well.
   b) ☐ to know they have a skill.
   c) ☐ special help.
   d) ☐ self-confidence.

6. Jevin's experience is that to enjoy a country you …
   a) ☐ have to adopt its ways and become part of it.
   b) ☐ must forget the one you were born in.
   c) ☐ should find work and meet people.
   d) ☐ need to know the language first.

7. Details about the test are …
   a) ☐ updated every year. b) ☐ difficult to find.
   c) ☐ only found on websites. d) ☐ not just online.

Post-listening

Task 47 If you would like to see how good your knowledge is about the UK, try taking the citizenship test after completing the listening task.
There are many websites which allow you to do this for free, for example: http://www.theuktest.com/life-in-the-uk-test.

The hazards of overpopulation

Pre-listening

Task 48

What do you think are the "hazards of overpopulation"? Mark the most appropriate definition with a cross (✗).

a) ☐ The rising number of young and old people on the whole planet.

b) ☐ The risk of losing too many people from a country.

c) ☐ The danger that comes with the growing number of people.

d) ☐ The recent trend towards people living in cities.

Task 49

The **bold** printed words are relevant vocabulary for the recording. Can you find out what they mean? Choose from the list of German words and fill in the correct letter. There are two more words than you need.

1: Abbau • **2:** unbedeutend • **3:** unausweichlich • **4:** Grenzertragsböden **5:** Anbaufläche • **6:** unverhältnismäßig • **7:** Sterben • **8:** Vielfalt • **9:** vielschichtig

a) One large concern is ozone **depletion** since the loss of this protective layer is responsible for climatic change. **1**

b) A loss of bio**diversity** means having fewer animal species and plant types. ____

c) The land which is not ideal for growing crops is known as **marginal land**. ____

d) A **disproportional** impact is when the effects of something affect people in very different ways. ____

e) Hundreds of years ago plagues caused a huge number of **die-offs**, in some cases killing whole communities. ____

f) In his first year at the bank they only let him do the **trivial** jobs. ____

g) The result of our constant pollution of nature will lead to an **inevitable** catastrophe. ____

While listening – Getting to know the text

Task 50 T 2

You will hear the beginning of an interview. Listen carefully and fill in the gaps with the missing words.

a) Have the environmental problems followed __________ what you thought?

b) The book that I wrote was ____________ on what happens in population.

c) We didn't know whether it [the climate] was gonna be _____________ or _____________.

d) So, the things that have been coming up have been much worse than we ____________.

Task 51 T 3

You will hear an interview concerning overpopulation. While listening, mark with a cross (✗) whether the statement is true or false.

Tips

Read the statements very carefully before listening to the text.

- Be sure that you understand the statements completely. Think of possible ways of how the information in the text may be presented; for example, concerning a: Was there a lot of information about the subject after/before the book was written?
- Listen carefully for synonyms or synonymous phrases of words in the text and the statement (e.g. instead of "future generations" you could hear "children" or "grandchildren").

	True	False
a) A lot of information was unavailable when the book was written.	☐	☐
b) Scientists are quite happy about current developments.	☐	☐
c) Everyone in the world could be fed.	☐	☐
d) Cities originally developed where farming land was poor.	☐	☐
e) Paul Ehrlich dislikes the present situation of having rich and poor societies.	☐	☐
f) Ehrlich believes that what we are doing today will benefit future generations.	☐	☐
g) Solving financial problems is not the same as solving environmental ones.	☐	☐

While listening – Matura-style task

Task 52

T 3

Read the information in the two lists carefully for 45 seconds, then listen to the text twice. While listening, match the beginning of each sentence (A–H) to the correct ending (1–10).
There are two sentence endings which are not used. Write your answers in the correct space. After you have listened twice to the text, give yourself another 45 seconds to check your answers.

Tips

A few guiding steps to help you deal with **Matching** exercises:

- Read through the task very carefully and mark the words/phrases that you might want to focus on while you are listening (e. g. "40 years", "climatic problems" etc.).
- Look at the sentence halves and see if you can already guess what kind of combinations are grammatically and logically possible (e. g. B: "Climatic problems have …" can only match with 3, 7 or 9); you can mark those options in the same colours.
- Usually the statements are in chronological order according to the information in the main text.
- When you have connected all the sentences, check that the remaining parts really are the "distractors".

A The book that he wrote 40 years ago …
B Climatic problems have …
C Extremes of weather will seriously …
D Famine …
E Farming is being …
F One criticism is that humans don't …
G The predictions made for the world's population …
H To reverse the damage now …

1 are not very good.
2 isn't caused by a lack of food in the world.
3 been made more efficient.
4 is seen as more or less impossible.
5 could be seen as positive.
6 was correct about population.
7 pushed further away from the fertile river valleys.
8 organise themselves properly.
9 arrived sooner than expected.
10 affect agriculture.

A	B	C	D	E	F	G	H

Inside the White House: The kitchen garden

Pre-listening

Task 53 Study the title of the topic. Which of the following words would you expect to hear in it? Mark the words which you think are probable.

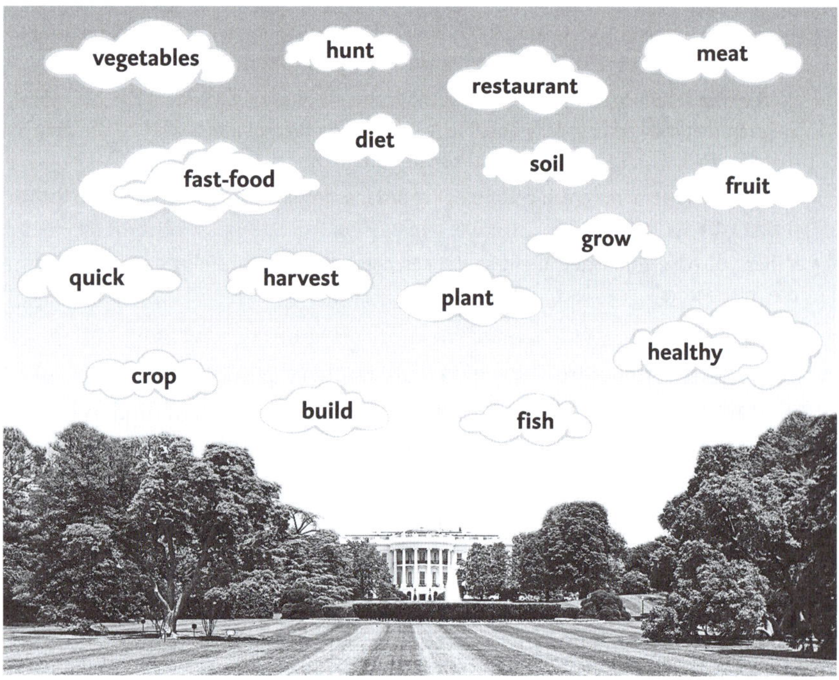

Task 54 Some words used in the audio text are probably new to you. Look at the sentences below and find the English word you require from the list and by completing the crossword. The German translations (in brackets) may help you here. You should also be able to recognise which of the words are verbs, adjectives, adverbs or nouns.

till • uniformly • fertility • amendment
eliminate[d] • establish • harvest • processed • ambassador

Down

1 '… similar' means things look the same. *(gleichmäßig)*
2 An … was sent to represent the school. *(Botschafter)*
3 There were no more problems because they had been …. *(beseitigen)*
4 The … of the ground influences how well plants grow. *(Fruchtbarkeit)*
5 The … is the crops when they are taken out of the ground. *(Ernte)*

Across

6 The first … is the initial digging over of the soil in preparation to plant things. *(Feldbestellung)*
7 She needed to add some … (s) to her diet and eat more healthily. *(Zusatz)*
8 It took some time to … the garden because a lot of work had to be done first before plants could grow in it. *(aufbauen)*
9 Tins of vegetables and frozen pizzas are examples of … food. *(verarbeitet)*

While listening – Getting to know the text

Task 55 T4

You will hear a report about a project in the White House begun by Michelle Obama and the White House's chef, Sam Kass.
While listening to Michelle Obama's introduction, mark all the boxes which you think are true with a cross (✗).

a) ☐ Michelle Obama's decision was a spontaneous reaction.
b) ☐ She was looking for a new hobby.
c) ☐ She realised that her family were not eating in the best way possible.
d) ☐ She started making the family eat out together once or twice a week.
e) ☐ She took many small steps which all helped her goal.
f) ☐ She hoped she would become a role model for other families.
g) ☐ She believed a First Lady must play an active role in American society.

Task 56 T5

Listen to the recording once and decide which of the statements are true and which are false. Mark the correct boxes with a cross (✗).

	True	False
a) The recording is about the gardens of the White House.	☐	☐
b) Michelle Obama wanted her family to eat more healthily.	☐	☐
c) Her first task was to prepare an area of land.	☐	☐
d) It was the first time in more than 100 years that she'd created a large productive garden.	☐	☐
e) The first crops were expected in autumn.	☐	☐
f) The children were very excited by the project.	☐	☐

While listening – Matura-style task

Task 57

T5

Before you start listening to the recording, you have 45 seconds to read the unfinished sentences. Then listen to the recording twice.
While listening, fill in the gaps using no more than four words.
After you have listened to the recording for the second time, give yourself 45 seconds to check your answers.

Tips

Short-answer tasks where you have to put in **a maximum of four words** are very common in the "Matura". Here are a few helpful hints that might be useful when dealing with these tasks:

- Read the tasks carefully and mark names and key words before you start listening.
- Try to listen to synonyms or synonymous phrases in the recording; but be careful: they might be used in a completely different context.
- Look at the sentences to see what kind of words would fit with the beginning (e.g. after an auxiliary verb there is usually a verb or a noun phrase; see example a).
- Write down the information that relates to the task (on an extra sheet) during the first listening; check your answers during the second listening and give the information in four words; often you will have to find paraphrases.

The first sentence (a) has already been done for you.

a) Michelle Obama thinks that she, her husband and the kids were ______
a busy working family.

b) She just changed little things, but soon Mrs Obama could see ______
______

c) The soil in the White House garden ______

d) The first gardening task is to increase the ______

e) There hasn't been a large productive garden ______

f) Thomas Jefferson had a great influence on the ______

g) There is a trend these days that people think about ______

h) Sam Kass finds the pupils' enthusiasm to be ______

i) It's easier to influence children's behaviour ______

j) President Obama eats ______

How government influences behaviour in society

Pre-listening

Task 58 Which photographs show how the government is trying to influence what people do? Mark these with a cross (✗).

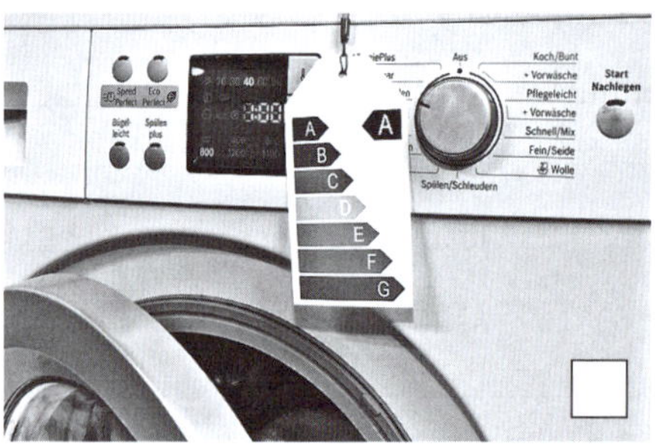

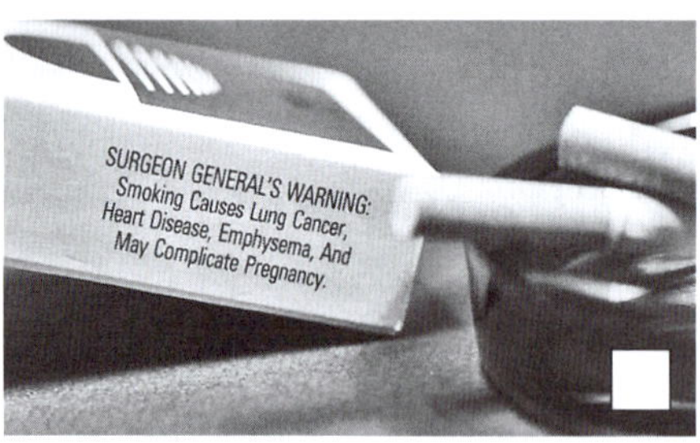

Task 59

You will hear the following words in the listening text in this order. Study the list carefully, then match each English word (A–I) to its German meaning (1–9). The example sentences below will help you work out which are the correct words.

A behavioural	**1** *Anstoß*
B intervention	**2** *Eingreifen*
C nudge	**3** *Fachkenntnis*
D rumble strip	**4** *Rüttelstreifen*
E fiscal	**5** *Finanz-*
F expertise	**6** *persönlich*
G array	**7** *Sozialwissenschaftler(in)*
H in person	**8** *Spektrum*
I social scientist	**9** *Verhaltens-*

A	B	C	D	E	F	G	H	I

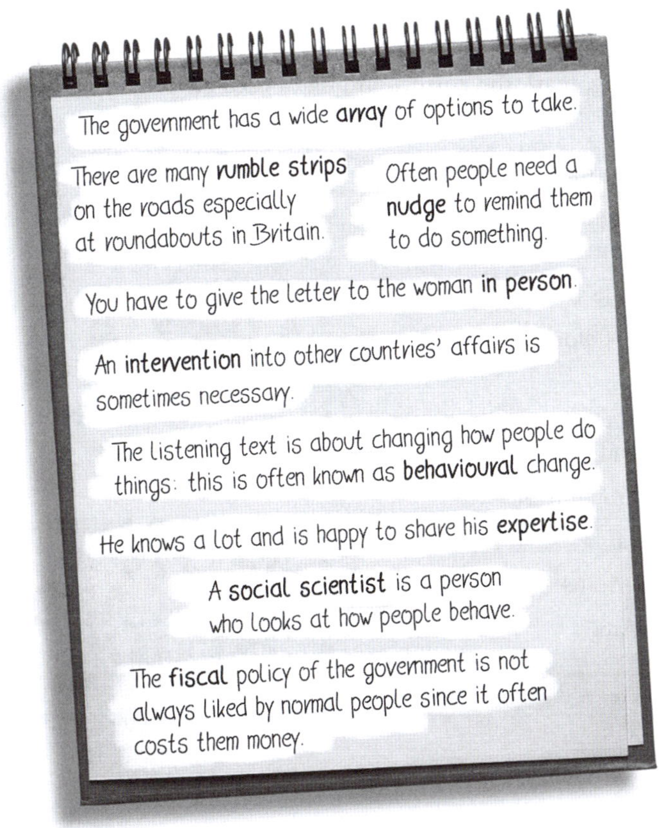

While listening – Getting to know the text

Task 60

T 6

Listen to this extract from the text. Complete the summary of it by filling in the gaps with words from the text.

Governments want to ______________ people's behaviour, for example, by getting them to use their ______________ less. They do this by something called nudges. Three examples of nudges are:

- rumble strips that make drivers ______________,
- ______________ which are altered to make people do something,
- and product placement in ______________ to persuade people to buy some things more than others.

While listening – Matura-style tasks

Task 61

T 7

You will hear someone talking about behavioural change intervention by the government.
Read the options available for 45 seconds, then listen to the recording twice. While listening, mark the correct ending to each sentence (a, b, c or d) with a cross (✗).

1. The government is concerned about …
   - a) ☐ people's weight and their alcohol consumption.
   - b) ☐ young people's drinking habits.
   - c) ☐ the health of older people.
   - d) ☐ living costs.

2. The concept of 'nudges' comes from …
   - a) ☐ the government itself.
   - b) ☐ economists.
   - c) ☐ some Americans.
   - d) ☐ psychologists.

3. Nudges are preferred as an alternative to …
   a) ☐ fines and punishments.
   b) ☐ laws.
   c) ☐ official warnings.
   d) ☐ educational campaigns.

4. Some slogans are very effective …
   a) ☐ to get people to change what they do.
   b) ☐ but only over a short time period.
   c) ☐ in changing people.
   d) ☐ because people remember them.

5. The committee intends to …
   a) ☐ issue a report to the government.
   b) ☐ research the problem further.
   c) ☐ force the government to take action.
   d) ☐ demand change.

6. Governments work together with …
   a) ☐ local people.
   b) ☐ various industries.
   c) ☐ supermarket chains.
   d) ☐ civil servants.

Task 62

T7

Read the information given here very carefully for 45 seconds, then listen to the text twice. While listening, match the beginning of each sentence (A–G) to the correct ending (1–9). There are two sentence endings which are not used. Write your answers in the correct space.
After you have listened to the text twice, give yourself another 45 seconds to check your answers.

A The government influences …

B Some changes in people's actions can be made by …

C The group looking at how the government achieved these soft nudges listened to …

D Nudges alone will not bring about major change; …

E One example of a successful government intervention concerned …

F From the committee's research it became clear that …

G A more effective way to label food than the government's is …

1 health education.

2 the opinions of a wide range of people.

3 gentle advertising campaigns.

4 an aspect of motoring.

5 the way society is.

6 non-political advisers are essential.

7 to have a colour system.

8 taking simple steps to force them to co-operate.

9 a combination of simultaneous actions is needed.

A	B	C	D	E	F	G

Taking the thug out of thug life

Pre-listening

Task 63

"Taking the thug (German: 'Schläger', 'Rowdy') out of thug life" involves a report concerning gang members in Los Angeles. Which sentence would you expect to be a summary of the recording?

a) ☐ Criminals leaving their street gangs by themselves.
b) ☐ Gang culture and how important it is in certain areas of Los Angeles.
c) ☐ An initiative helping members leave their gangs and that culture.
d) ☐ A government analysis of the gangs in downtown Los Angeles.

Task 64

In the Matura-style task at the end of this topic you are asked to complete sentences while listening to the recording. The words to fill in the gaps are usually not exactly the same as those you are going to hear.
Look at the sentences (a–f) below, then "re-word" each underlined section so that you can complete the gap in no more than four words.
The first one (a) has already been done as an example for you.

a) Many gang members have experienced friends and family being murdered and they wish to escape from this environment.
Many gang members want to change *their way of life.*

b) Young people sometimes believe they have no other alternative but to join a gang.
Some people believe that they ____________ in a certain way.

c) Walking alone in the dark at night isn't advisable in many cities.
If you are by yourself, it's better to be safe and not to ____________
____________.

d) People who have been in prison often have problems finding work afterwards.
Frequently employers are not interested in giving ____________
____________.

e) You may think body piercing and tattoos look good but other people may think differently, even if you are a really nice person.
_______________ is just as important as someone's character for many people.

f) Many programmes are winning the fight against gang membership by helping young people to leave gangs and become normal members of society.
Many programmes _______________ in what they are doing.

While listening – Getting to know the text

Task 65 T8

Listen to the recording (which is the beginning of the text) and match the names (A–D) with the corresponding information (1–6). There are two more numbers than you need.

A Elizabeth Lee
B Kevin
C Kevin's best friend
D Gregory Boyle

1 is a gang leader.
2 founded Homeboy Industries.
3 reports on Homeboy Industries.
4 is dead.
5 killed Kevin's father.
6 now works in the food industry.

A	B	C	D

While listening – Matura-style tasks

Task 66

T 9

Listen to the report about escaping from gang life in Los Angeles. The report involves many speakers.
Study the task for 45 seconds, then listen to the recording twice. While listening, mark the correct ending to each sentence (a, b, c or d) with a cross (✗).
After the second listening give yourself another 45 seconds to check your answers before looking at the key to see if you are right.

1. The programme in Los Angeles …
   a) ☐ started with hundreds of gangs.
   b) ☐ began because it is the gang capital of the world.
   c) ☐ has become a role model for other places.
   d) ☐ had difficulties initially.

2. Father Gregory Boyle's philosophy is to …
   a) ☐ keep gangs apart so they take responsibility for their own territories.
   b) ☐ make gang members mix by having them work together.
   c) ☐ find work for gang members so they do not get bored.
   d) ☐ encourage competition between rival gangs.

3. Greg Boyle believes that every gang member basically wants to …
   a) ☐ stay on the programme as long as possible.
   b) ☐ be a success.
   c) ☐ have a meaningful job.
   d) ☐ have a normal life.

4. The programme aims to …
   a) ☐ send people back to high school.
   b) ☐ develop ex-gang members' social skills.
   c) ☐ provide people with an education and work-related skills.
   d) ☐ build up gang members' self-confidence.

5. There are many reasons why people join gangs, however …
   a) ☐ the main cause is poverty.
   b) ☐ being in one provides a sense of security.
   c) ☐ friends are the biggest influence.
   d) ☐ having a 'cool' image and gaining respect are the most important.

6. Many gang members …
   a) ☐ have to become aggressive to survive.
   b) ☐ unfortunately return to crime after completing the programme.
   c) ☐ find their family and friends support them.
   d) ☐ would prefer not to be in one.

Task 67 T9

Read the following questions carefully before listening to the text. Use no more than four words to give a short answer to each question. The first one (a) has been done for you.

a) What is Los Angeles known as?
   United States' gang capital

b) Why are other countries interested in the anti-gang programme?
   ____

c) Who did Kevin see killed?
   ____

d) What starts to break down during the 18 months of the programme?
   ____

e) What can improve people's job prospects?
   ____

f) When did the programme begin and by whom was it started?
   when: _______________; by whom: _______________

g) Which factor is the most influential one making people join gangs?
   ____

h) What was the reporter's first reaction when she met the gang members?
   ____

American icons: Georgia O'Keeffe's skull paintings

Pre-listening

Task 68

Which is the best definition of an icon in your opinion?
Mark the box with a cross (✗).

a) ☐ a person who has become famous and is very rich and influential
b) ☐ an era that is defined in a special way through style or a historical event
c) ☐ a person or object that has become a symbol of something and typifies it
d) ☐ an image or picture that everyone knows and instantly recognises

Task 69

You will hear the underlined words in the listening text. What would you expect them to mean? Mark the most suitable option with a cross (✗).

1. O'Keeffe grew up on a <u>dairy</u> farm.

a) ☐

b) ☐

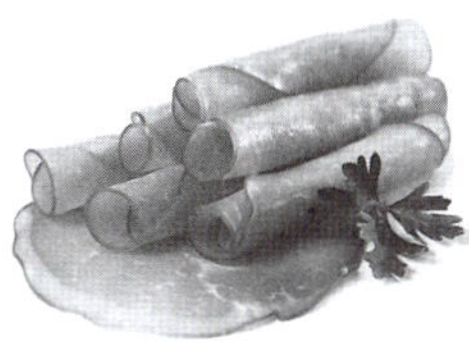
c) ☐

2. She lived during the <u>roaring</u> twenties in New York.
   a) ☐ exciting
   b) ☐ boring
   c) ☐ expensive

3. She had a <u>rocky</u> marriage.

a) ☐

b) ☐

c) ☐

4. She had a good <u>confidante</u> who she could trust.

a) ☐ friend

b) ☐ horse

c) ☐ dog

5. She lived in a <u>hacienda</u> in New Mexico.

a) ☐

b) ☐

c) ☐

While listening – Getting to know the text

Task 70

T 10

In matching exercises you have to deal with many options that seem probable at first glance. Look at some ways in which you can reduce the number of matching options.

Listen to the short excerpts from the audio text. You should stop the recording after every section to do the exercise. Match the start of each sentence to its correct ending and then explain your choice. Note down key words that support your choice below the correct solution <u>and</u> explain why the other two endings are false.

The first one (0) has been done for you.

0. At first O'Keeffe …

a) ☐ worked on a farm.

O'Keeffe grew up on a farm – she didn't work on one.

b) ☒ was a teacher.

She taught school (in Texas).

c) ☐ lived in Texas.

She worked in Texas but was born ("grew up") in Wisconsin.

1. O'Keeffe went to New Mexico ...
   a) ☐ to see friends in Taos.
   b) ☐ because of personal problems.
   c) ☐ and received an invitation there.

2. She wanted to keep ...
   a) ☐ people interested in the weather.
   b) ☐ everything different.
   c) ☐ the area a secret from other people.

3. Her collection of rocks and bones ...
   a) ☐ help her to paint her pictures.
   b) ☐ were carefully selected.
   c) ☐ had no initial purpose.

4. O'Keeffe would have been very happy ...
   a) ☐ if the critic had written something about the bones.
   b) ☐ with the positive reviews of the critic.
   c) ☐ to have feminism recognised in her art.

While listening – Matura-style tasks

Task 71

T11

Listen to a report about the American artist, Georgia O'Keeffe.
Match the beginning of each sentence (A–F) to the correct ending (1–8). There are two sentence endings which are not used.
Write your answers in the table below.

Tips

- Before you listen to the recording check if there are any sentence combinations which could be possible (grammatically and logically).
- Cross out an ending when you have used it.

A At the height of the fashionable 1920s, O'Keeffe …
B The effect of New Mexico …
C An invitation …
D In New Mexico she immediately …
E O'Keeffe's new work …
F From a very early age O'Keeffe …

1 knew what she wanted to do.
2 reflected the area well.
3 was to radically influence her work.
4 exhibited her paintings.
5 was living in New York.
6 was a turning point in her life.
7 felt she belonged.
8 didn't really work hard.

A	B	C	D	E	F

Task 72

T 12

You will hear the rest of the report about Georgia O'Keeffe.
Read the unfinished sentences first, then listen to the recording.
While listening, fill in the gaps using no more than four words.
Listen to the report a second time and check your answers, completing any sections that you missed out at first.

a) O'Keeffe viewed her collection of objects as things …

____

b) Her first New Mexico inspired paintings came from the objects …

____

c) Her first painting was of …

____

d) O'Keeffe criticised many people for pretending to …

____

e) She didn't like how the critics viewed her work on the basis of …

____

f) In her work she was trying to achieve …

____

Key
Lösungsvorschläge

Tipps zum Lösungsteil

Der Lösungsteil bietet Ihnen zum einen die Möglichkeit, Ihre Antworten zu überprüfen – die korrekten Lösungsvorschläge sind hierbei immer **in Farbe** angegeben. Darüber hinaus erhalten Sie auch weiterführende Hinweise und alternative Lösungen. Sie sollten deshalb:

- die Lösungen als Hilfestellung sehen, die Sie bei der Prüfungsvorbereitung unterstützen soll,
- wenn Sie Probleme bei einer Aufgabe haben, erst die mit Raute ◆ gekennzeichneten Hinweise lesen, die Ihnen u. a. die exakte Textstelle aufzeigen, an der sich die Lösung befindet,
- die Transkripte zu den Hörtexten erst nachschlagen, wenn Sie ein „Topic" abgeschlossen haben oder wenn sich die Antwort trotz Hinweis und Lösung noch nicht klar erschlossen hat.

Reading Comprehension

Topic 1: Advertising for kids

Task 1

A	B	C	D	E	F	G	H	I	J
1	6	10	9	7	5	8	2	4	3

Task 2 **Do you hate adverts?**

All media, TV and the printed press, are heavily **dependent** on advertising revenue. Newspapers need money to **finance** costs, which include paper, printing, distribution and, last but not least, salaries for editors, journalists, designers, cartoonists and photographers.

Publishers earn the necessary funds by selling space for **adverts** in the paper. Television channels cover costs by selling time for **commercials** which are broadcast in **breaks** during programmes. Many viewers are annoyed when the announcer interrupts the show with the phrase, “We’ll be back after a short break! Stay tuned.” To **avoid** viewers switching over to another **channel**, many advertisers try to make their commercials entertaining.

However, thanks to the progress in computer and Internet **technology**, another way of watching your favourite programmes has become available – and all of this independent of schedules set by the TV companies. Viewers can now **watch** films and videos whenever they want. Streaming is the key word. Programmes are transmitted via **cable** or over the Internet to users’ tablets, laptops or TV sets. Taking advantage of people’s aversion to adverts during programmes, new streaming platforms have been founded which do not **broadcast** commercials – at a cost, however. To enjoy advert-free television you have to subscribe to these streaming **services**.

Pay special attention to word classes in this exercise and how they match the given sentence structure (e.g. only an adjective will work in the first gap). Check the context again with the words you filled in.

Task 3 The overall purpose of the author is to …

a) ☐ warn adults about the health dangers of fatty foods.

b) ☐ advise parents on how to limit media consumption of their children.

c) ☐ describe how social media have changed our society.

d) ☒ inform readers about how advertisers influence young children.

Task 4

- firms use advertising as a means of promoting <u>public relations</u>. (line(s): **18/19**)

"firms themselves […] by <u>improving their image</u>" (ll. 18/19)

- young <u>children</u> are unable to <u>see through</u> the tricks of the advertisers. (line(s): **29/30**)

"<u>the very young</u> do not <u>understand</u> […] programmes." (ll. 29/30)

- parents want their children to eat <u>healthily</u>. (line(s): **33**)

"parents would like their kids to stick to a <u>nutritious diet</u>" (l. 33)

- fast-food restaurants will <u>substitute</u> fat and sugar with healthier substances. (line(s): **50/51**)

"healthier meals […] <u>replace</u> fatty and sugary ingredients" (ll. 50–52)

- <u>food producers</u> want to reduce the <u>danger</u> of young people becoming too fat. (line(s): **54/55**)

"<u>food industry</u>'s contribution to minimising the <u>risk</u> of overweight children and young people." (ll. 54/55)

Task 5

1. "product placement" (l. 24) means …
   a) ☐ displaying a product properly on the shelves in the supermarket.
   b) ☒ showing products in a film scene so that viewers see the brand name.
   c) ☐ stressing the importance of a product in adverts.

2. "persuasive intent of adverts" (l. 29) means …
   a) ☒ adverts want to make you buy a product.
   b) ☐ adverts emphasise the quality of a product.
   c) ☐ adverts inform you about a product.

3. "low-nutrition foods" (l. 35) means …
   a) ☐ food with little or no calories.
   b) ☐ food which keeps blood sugar levels down.
   c) ☒ food which is not very healthy (junk food).

Task 6

0	1	2	3	4	5	6	7	8
K	D	G	A	J	H	B	C	E

Option F ("Children watch too much TV") is not correct, because the text only mentions how many hours children watch TV; the author does not judge whether children spend too many hours in front of the box.
Option I ("Companies need advertising to survive") is not correct, because it only says in the text that adverts are necessary and help firms to sell more.

Task 7 Part 1:

0 In our digital age media consumption is steadily on the increase, with the Internet, social networks and television taking first place across generations. Psychologists and educators have often pointed out that children represent a particularly captive audience. (A)

1 Recent studies in the USA reveal that young people aged 8 to 18 spend an average of more than seven hours daily using some kind of entertainment media. Consequently, all sorts of businesses, large and small, take advantage of the extensive media usage and spend enormous amounts of money targeting children with commercials. According to market researchers children aged 2–11 watch more than 25,000 advertisements a year on TV alone, a figure that does not include product placement and concealed advertising in TV shows and films. (B)

2 There is general agreement that advertising is necessary because it helps firms to boost sales and thus generates jobs – not least in the advertising agencies which create the ads and commercials. In addition, it helps finance not only TV programmes, but also cultural and sporting events, many of which could not be staged without donations from industry. It goes without saying that the firms themselves profit to a certain degree from sponsoring by improving their image, but especially in the arts and entertainment sector the investment does not usually yield returns. (C), (D)

3 The food industry is one of the biggest spenders on the advertising market and has developed special strategies to market foods and beverages to children on television, on the Internet, on mobile phones, in magazines, through product placement in movies and video games. In addition, adverts appear on product packages, on clothing and other merchandise, and almost anywhere where a logo or product image can be shown, too.

4 More often than not, these advertisements have a greater influence on children's choice of food than what the parents tell their children to eat; especially the very young do not understand the persuasive intent of adverts and cannot distinguish between advertising and programmes. Parents complain that aggressive food marketers undermine their authority, because adverts give children a completely different view of what is healthy to eat. Whereas parents would like their kids to stick to a nutritious diet by eating vegetables, fruit and salads, food adverts aimed at children mostly promote low-nutrition foods full of fat and sugar. **(E)**

5 For a long time, the health authorities have appealed to food and beverage companies, stores, broadcasters and schools to market foods responsibly to children. This means that, above all, they should support parents' efforts to foster healthy eating habits in children, banning all adverts which might be harmful to the mental and physical health of the younger generation. **(F)**

6 These appeals seem to be bearing fruit as a change in the advertising strategies of several major companies is taking place. In cooperation with the government and citizen action groups, they have worked out and agreed on guidelines for food marketing to children in order to avoid the negative effect on children's well-being. Fast-food chains, for example, have committed themselves to limiting advertising aimed at children younger than 12 to food and drinks that meet strict nutritional guidelines. **(G)**

7 In addition, for children under 12 years old they will offer special Kids Meals that provide no more than 560 calories per meal and have less than 30 per cent calories from fat and no added trans fats. New and healthier meals for children are being developed that will replace fatty and sugary ingredients. The companies will use organic unsweetened apple sauce, low-fat milk and fresh apple slices. **(H)**

8 These measures are seen as the fast food industry's contribution to minimising the risk of overweight children and young people. Unfortunately recent studies within the industry have frequently shown that some food and beverage companies do not abide by the rules they had agreed on. **(I)**

Part 2:

1. Firms spend a lot of money on …
   a) ☐ TV adverts which tell parents what to buy for their children.
   b) ☐ adverts which entertain parents and children.
   c) ☐ commercials which fascinate younger and older audiences.
   d) ☒ commercials which are meant especially for young children.

In the text it says, "businesses […] spend enormous amounts of money targeting children with commercials" (ll. 7–9).

2. The money with which firms sponsor theatre and opera productions …
   a) ☐ is a bad investment.
   b) ☐ pays off because it makes sales boost.
   c) ☒ is often not profitable.
   d) ☐ is now more necessary than ever.

In the text it says, "the investment does not usually yield returns" (l. 20).

3. The adverts which children watch on TV …
   a) ☐ give a totally wrong picture of family life.
   b) ☒ make children want to eat the wrong food.
   c) ☐ are completely different from their own experience.
   d) ☐ make kids ask their parents for more and more toys.

In the text it says, "adverts give children a completely different view of what is healthy to eat" (ll. 31/32).

4. The aim of the new guidelines is to …
   a) ☐ make children eat the right kind of food.
   b) ☒ make the industry offer healthier food for kids.
   c) ☐ ban TV food adverts which are directed at children.
   d) ☐ tell parents what is good and healthy for their kids.

In the text it says, "guidelines […] to avoid the negative effect on children's well-being" (ll. 44/45).

5. The new guidelines for healthier food for children …
   a) ☒ are not observed by all companies.
   b) ☐ must be improved by the authorities.
   c) ☐ have to be agreed on by more firms.
   d) ☐ have to be controlled by more studies.

In the text it says, "some food and beverage companies do not abide by the rules" (ll. 56/57).

Topic 2: Columbus – Adventurer across unknown seas

Task 8

A	B	C	D	E	F	G	H	I	J	K	L
2	7	8	12	3	10	1	4	11	6	9	5

Task 9

October 12, 1492 marks the day of the arrival of Christopher Columbus on American shores after an almost endless **voyage** across unknown seas. The day of his landing was the end of a remarkable **enterprise** and the beginning of an **exchange** of people and cultures between two different worlds. Columbus Day or Discovery Day has a special meaning in the United States and in **numerous** Latin American countries. Some see Columbus' **deed** in a positive light, whereas others **reject** this positive appreciation. Many Native Americans **perceive** the arrival of the Europeans as a catastrophe, because Columbus' **discovery** opened the door for the invasion of the North American continent by immigrants from the Old World. The influx of pioneers and settlers during the period of the westward movement changed the **destiny** of the indigenous population profoundly. There is a common **belief** that the white man is responsible for the extinction of many tribes and the **destruction** of Indian culture. Today Native Americans work for a process to reawaken old traditions by teaching the younger generation about their forefathers in special tribal schools and at universities.

Task 10

1. "unyielding" (l. 20)
   - a) ☐ insufficient
   - b) ☐ unprepared
   - c) ☐ impatient
   - d) ☒ resolute
2. "revolutionary" (l. 41)
   - a) ☐ unknown
   - b) ☐ upsetting
   - c) ☒ unheard of
   - d) ☐ tragic
3. "lingering" (l. 54)
   - a) ☐ complete
   - b) ☐ unreasonable
   - c) ☒ lasting
   - d) ☐ final

Task 11

1. Which of these countries is not mentioned in the text?

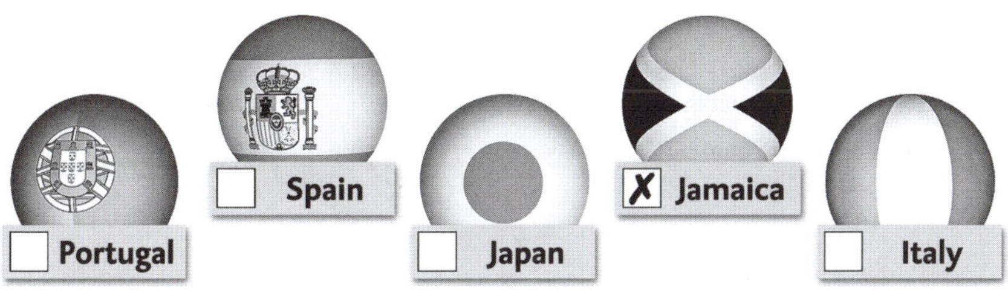

2. List the islands which are mentioned in the text.
   Madeira, Azores, (Japan), Guanahaní, (Bahamas), San Salvador, Cuba
   Strictly speaking, Japan and the Bahamas actually consist of several islands.

3. Which adjectives describe the character of Columbus best?
   a) ☐ uneducated b) ☒ studious c) ☐ greedy
   d) ☒ daring e) ☐ incompetent f) ☒ wilful

Task 12

	1	A	C	C	O	M	P	L	I	S	**H**	M	E	N	T	
						2	C	R	E	D	**I**	T				
							3	A	B	U	**S**	E				
										4	**P**	E	R	C	E	I	V	E
										5	**A**	C	Q	U	I	R	E	
								6	C	O	**N**	D	E	M	N	
						7	C	O	N	V	**I**	N	C	E		
									8	C	**O**	N	D	U	C	T
				9	F	E	R	T	I	**L**	E				
								10	M	E	**A**	S	L	E	S	

Solution: **Hispaniola**

Task 13

Statement	True	False	First four words
a) Columbus based his voyage on the tales of other seafarers.	☒	☐	**Having often heard reports**
b) Columbus had no trust in the seaworthiness of the vessels of his time.	☐	☒	**According to his calculations**
c) Columbus was stripped of his post because he could not bring home enough gold.	☒	☐	**He was received enthusiastically**
d) Finding a route to India was less significant than the discovery of America.	☒	☐	**What Columbus did not**
e) When Columbus started his voyage most people in Europe believed that the earth was a sphere.	☐	☒	**Columbus conducted his enterprise**
f) Some people see Columbus' achievement in a very negative light.	☒	☐	**The fact that some**

g) Columbus was the first and only discoverer of the North American continent.	☐	☒	**Yet it would be**
h) Columbus was always convinced he had found a new continent.	☐	☒	**Christopher Columbus died on**

Hinweise:

a *"Having often heard reports of legendary westward voyages [...] Columbus studied old books and charts" (ll. 13–15)*

b *"a distance that could be sailed in existing ships." (ll. 18/19)*

c *"lost the support of the monarchs as he failed to find the gold they had hoped for and was replaced as governor general" (ll. 28/29)*

d *"the discovery he was to make would be more important and valuable than the route he failed to find." (ll. 32–34)*

e *"at a time when Europe was just awakening from the Dark Ages, leaving behind the belief that the earth was flat and stood at the centre of the planetary system" (ll. 35–39)*

f *"some see Columbus' arrival as a positive event, whereas others condemn it as the beginning of a genocide" (ll. 52/53)*

g *"Yet it would be just as unfair [...] to credit him alone for the expansion of the Old World." (ll. 54–56)*

h *"Christopher Columbus died on May 20, 1506, [...] still believing that he had reached Asia." (ll. 58/59)*

Task 14

a) How did Columbus find out more information about voyages beyond the Azores?

studied maps and charts

The answer "heard reports of/about voyages" (ll. 13/14) is not correct, because in the question it says "more information".

b) What did Columbus try to find west of Portugal?

a route to Asia/the way to Asia/Asia/Japan/west route to Japan

In the text it says that Columbus made a "proposal to search for a route to Asia". (l. 20)

c) Where did Columbus think he had landed when he arrived on Guanahaní?

in the East Indies/in India/in Asia

"because he believed he had reached the East Indies." (ll. 25/26)

d) How long did Columbus' first voyage last?
8 months/from August to March
"On August 3, 1492, three small and simple ships set sail [...] and arrived back in Spain in March 1493." (ll. 22–27)

e) What began between Europe and America after Columbus' discovery?
an exchange of goods/trade/the Columbian Exchange
"initiated an exchange between the New and Old Worlds of food, plants and animals, of inventions and cultural, religious and political concepts" (ll. 42/43)

f) In which way was the health of the native population affected?
infectious diseases and epidemics
"transmission of infectious diseases, such as measles, which caused epidemics and led to the nearly complete destruction of the peoples of the newfound lands" (ll. 46–48)

g) How did the Europeans treat the natives?
abused and exploited them
"The colonists abused the natives, exploiting them cruelly as slaves." (ll. 48/49)

h) How did the Europeans destroy the livelihood of the Native Americans?
robbed their land/drove them away
"They robbed them of their land, driving them away into the less fertile areas, decimating their population." (ll. 49/50)

Topic 3: Working children

Task 15

Jumbled word	Solution	German
VILELETA	**alleviate**	erleichtern
EUCDT	**deduct**	abziehen
ORU	**pour**	strömen
LPNOXTTIIOA	**exploitation**	Ausbeutung
AETRNM	**garment**	Bekleidung
LLI	**mill**	Fabrik; Mühle
TRYA	**stray**	verlorengegangen, heruntergefallen
UCEINTEBSS	**subsistence**	Existenz, Lebensunterhalt
TWPESHOA	**sweatshop**	Ausbeutungsbetrieb

Task 16

Although slavery is against the **law** everywhere, it continues to exist in many parts of the world. Especially in Asian and African **developing** countries people of all ages are exploited as cheap **labour**. The term 'slavery' is rarely used anymore. Instead, slavery is usually referred to as 'bonded labour' or 'human trafficking.' From the 17th to the 19th **century** mainly British and Dutch ships made slave trading voyages between the continents of Europe, Africa and America. Because of the horrible conditions on the ships many black Africans died on the journey. In Louisiana and Mississippi the Africans worked in the hot and **sticky** climate on the cotton fields of the white plantation **owners**. The same tragedy happened on the other side of the world. South Pacific islanders were kidnapped from their **villages** and used as slaves on the **cotton** and sugar cane plantations of Queensland, Australia. The brutal and shameful practice became known as 'blackbirding'. Today most bonded labourers work in agriculture, the service industry and in **factories**. In the textile **mills** in some Asian countries even **tiny** children are exposed to **unsafe** working conditions and can be fired – also called **sacked** – from their jobs for no reason at all.

Task 17

The text "Working children" is primarily about …

a) ☐ the misery of working children during the Industrial Revolution.
b) ☐ working children in England, India and Australia.
c) ☒ the situation of working children in the past and the present.
d) ☐ the improvements in the situation of working children.

Task 18

Name	Age	Country	Workplace	Job
William	**11**	**England**	**cotton mill**	**pick up stray cotton**
James	**9**	**England**	**coal mine**	**push truck of coal**
Hamza	**10**	**India (New Delhi)**	**garment workshop**	**sew logos onto baby T-shirts**
Amitab	**12**	**India**	**stone quarry**	**load stones onto lorries**

Task 19

Statement	True	False	First four words
a) There were no fixed working hours for William.	X		**He usually works from**
b) William operated a machine to weave cloth in the textile mill.		X	**As he is small**
c) Apart from James there was nobody in the family who earned any money.	X		**A catastrophe for his**
d) Hamza's employer bought the boy's family a small piece of land.		X	**He works here because**
e) Hamza and Amitab, who come from the same village and work in the same factory, are victims of exploitation.		X	**His friend Amitab, who**
f) The worldwide exchange of goods today is partly responsible for the problem of child labour.	X		**Campaigners against child labour**
g) Children in Asian factories often do not earn enough money to live on.	X		**To lower labour costs**

Hinweise:

a *cf. ll. 3/4*

b *cf. ll. 6–8*

c *cf. l. 13*

d *cf. ll. 17–20*

e *cf. ll. 22–24*

f *cf. ll. 41/42*

g *cf. ll. 42–45*

Task 20

a) Why was William unaware of <u>how long</u> he <u>worked</u> every day?

no clocks in factory

"There are no clocks in the mill, anyway." (l. 5)

b) Why was William especially useful for the job he had to do?

he was small

"As he is small, his job is to dive in and out of the machinery picking up bits of stray cotton." (ll. 6–8)

c) How did Hamza get into bonded labour?
(his) parents sold him
"He works here because his parents had to sell him to the factory owner in exchange for a loan so that they could keep their small piece of land, which belongs to the bank." (ll. 17–20)

d) Why was Amitab's job particularly harmful?
carry heavy stones / too heavy for child/hard physical work
"His friend Amitab [...] works in a quarry in Alwar, Rajasthan, loading heavy stones onto lorries." (ll. 22–24)

e) What effect did the Factory Acts have?
improved working conditions / alleviated exploitation
"their working conditions began to improve when a number of Factory Acts were passed by the British Parliament to alleviate the worst exploitation of women and children" (ll. 25–27)

Task 21

a) Amitab and Hamza come from India, which still counts as a **developing country**.
"Hamza and Amitab do not profit from these regulations because they live in a developing country." (ll. 37/38)

b) Global companies often use children as workers because they want to **lower labour costs / save money / make more profit**.
"To lower labour costs multinational corporations set up production plants in Asia where they employ children" (ll. 42–44)

c) Indications that the problem of child labour can be tackled successfully are, for example, **declining numbers / shown by the ILO / that numbers have declined**.
"According to the ILO (the International Labour Organization) the global number of child labourers has declined since 2000, from 246 million to 168 million children." (ll. 46–49)

d) One reason for the fact that the situation for children is improving is **stricter legislation / higher investments in education / investments in social protection**.
"This progress has been achieved by stricter legislation and higher investments in education and social protection" (ll. 49/50)

Topic 4: The secret of the mysterious crop field rings

Task 22 Many people like tales of **mystery (1)** and horror. Fantastic creatures like monsters and mutants appear in hundreds and thousands of comics, video games and films, thus generating substantial **funds (2)** for the entertainment industry. 19th century novelists created the characters of Frankenstein and Count Dracula, that are still very much alive and have made **numerous (3)** appearances in theatrical, film and television productions. Some weird creatures have even acquired cult status among **enthusiasts (4)**, such as the **"Alien" (5)**, an aggressive killer beast from the science fiction horror film series of the same name (1979–2012), whereas E.T. – short for **extraterrestrial (6)** – just wanted to call home (1984). Another favourite, Godzilla, the King of the Monsters, left its first **traces (7)** on Earth in a Japanese film from 1954 and made spectacular returns to the big screen, for example in 1998 and 2014. Reports of **sightings (8)** of unidentified flying objects (UFOs) make the headlines more or less regularly. As early as 1938 Orson Welles shocked the American public with his **ingenious (9)** radio adaptation of H.G. Wells' novel *The War of the Worlds*. Panic broke out because listeners really believed that flying **saucers (10)** had landed on our planet. Four years earlier, in 1934, an English newspaper printed a photo of "Nessie", the Loch Ness monster. Many people do not only believe in its existence, they are also **convinced (11)** that the **elaborate (12)** animal figures and geometrical designs in the Peruvian desert and in English **wheat (13)** fields are the works of an energy force from outer space. Be it as it may, the increasing amount of stories, novels, comics, videos and films featuring androids, replicants, monsters and mutants prove the popularity of people's belief in the unbelievable.

Task 23 What is the main text about?

a) ☐ The intensive scientific investigation of crop circles.

The text mentions that two M.P.s called for a scientific investigation of crop circles (cf. ll. 23/24), but it is not the main idea of the text.

b) ☐ The first appearance of a crop circle in an English wheat field.

In the text it only says that a crop circle was discovered in the 1980s and was reported in newspapers (cf. l. 10). It does not say that it was the first appearance of such a pictograph.

c) [X] The different theories about the origin of crop circles.

This statement summarises best the idea which takes up the greatest part of the text: the different opinions about who or what made the crop circles.

d) [ ] How to make a crop circle.

The text gives some details about how people made crops circles (cf. ll. 38–43), but it does not give instructions on how to make one.

Task 24

Statement	First four words
a) … the straw was **carefully formed into a ring on the ground.**	**The corn had been**
b) … the discovery of the farmer **quickly made the headlines.**	**He told the reporter**
c) … some people thought **aliens had made the circles.**	**Some attribut-ed the elaborate**
d) … the government was asked to **put up money for a proper examination.**	**To finally put an**

Hinweise:

a *"The corn had been neatly flattened into a large circular pattern" (ll. 7/8)*

b *"He told the reporter […] and it was soon reported nationwide" (ll. 10/11)*

c *"the circles were the work of intelligent beings from outer space" (ll. 16/17)*

d *"to finance a serious scientific investigation" (l. 24)*

Task 25

0	1	2	3	4	5	6
F	A	D	I	H	E	B

Hinweise:

0 *"On a bright sunny morning […] Jameson […] noticed something" (ll. 1/2)*

1 *"Some attributed the elaborate multi-circle designs to natural causes […] others saw them as the creations of hoaxers, and still others believed the circles were the work of intelligent beings from outer space." (ll. 14–17)*

2 *"The probe into the origin of the mysterious rings in the wheat fields continued. For many years" (ll. 19–21)*

3 *"To finally put an end to speculations two M.P.s called for the government to finance a serious scientific investigation" (ll. 23/24)*

4 *"Before they start their intricate work, many use computers, GPS equipment and lasers to help map out the ingenious patterns." (ll. 40–42)*

5 *"In 1978 Bower had to create his straight lines using a circular wire attached to his cap." (ll. 42/43)*

6 *"much to the frustration and anger of farmers, who do not want to have their fields invaded by crop circle enthusiasts" (ll. 48–50)*

Task 26

0	1	2	3	4	5	6
E	F	A	C	G	I	B

Hinweise:

0 *The pronoun "he" refers to "farmer Timothy Jameson". The word "something" can introduce a defining relative clause. The relative pronoun "that" can be omitted because it is not the subject of the clause. In the sentence farmer Jameson noticed something (that) "he had never seen before" (cf. ll. 2–4).*

1 *The word "large" (l. 8) is a hint to fill in the gap. The part provided (F) tells the reader more exactly how big the circle was. "The corn had been neatly flattened into a large circular pattern of about 30 metres in diameter." (ll. 7/8)*

2 *The words "studied" (l. 13) and "speculating" (l. 14) in the main text can be used best in connection with the term "debate" in the alternative provided (A).*

3 *The time adverbial "for many years" (ll. 20/21) is further explained by part C. Remember: For journalists the summer months are the "silly season" with little important news to report, so they are desperately looking for stories to interest their readers. Crop circle news fills the gap. "For many years during the summer months the papers were full of reports of new sightings" (ll. 20/21)*

4 *Option G supplies more information about what sort of investigation (cf. l. 24) was carried out. It is the only alternative which fits the sentence ("of about 30 metres in diameter" has already been used and does not make sense).*

5 *The preposition "on"(l. 35) in the main text can help you find the proper adverbial of place "the field in Headbourne Worthy" (I). It was the field of farmer Jameson (cf. l. 34), who is also mentioned in this sentence.*

6 *"not only" (l. 44) is the key word in this sentence asking for its complement "but (also)" (cf. B). "Even today hundreds of sophisticated crop circles still appear annually not only in southern England, but around the world." (ll. 43/44)*

Task 27

0. Farmer Jameson was surprised because …
   a) ☐ a huge spaceship had landed in his field.
   b) ☒ he saw a huge pattern in his field.
   c) ☐ his wheat field had been destroyed.
   d) ☐ the corn in his wheat field had been cut overnight.

cf. ll. 5–7

1. Farmer Jameson had no idea how the pattern had got in his field because …
   a) ☐ he had slept solidly and had not heard anything.
   b) ☐ he had never seen such a design before.
   c) ☒ he could not detect any traces on the ground.
   d) ☐ of the enormous size of the design.

cf. ll. 9/10

2. Scientists began to search for an explanation for the crop circles …
   a) ☐ after Farmer Jameson had told a reporter about his discovery.
   b) ☐ after the whole nation saw a report about it.
   c) ☒ after the discovery of numerous crop circles the following year.
   d) ☐ after an intervention from the government.

cf. ll. 11–13

3. Some people believed the crop circles were …
   a) ☒ made by people as a joke.
   b) ☐ made by farmers to attract visitors.
   c) ☐ the work of touring visitors.
   d) ☐ designed by astronauts.

cf. ll. 14–17

4. Eventually, two artists admitted that they had made the circles because …
   a) ☐ a journalist had discovered their secret.
   b) ☐ a reporter had published photographs showing the men in action.
   c) ☒ they didn't want the government to waste money on an investigation.
   d) ☐ they were no longer interested in contracting circles.

cf. ll. 25–28

Topic 5: Cyber Crime

Task 28

0	1	2	3	4	5	6	7	8	9	10
G	E	H	C	D	J	A	I	K	F	B

Task 29

								0	C	H	E	A	T		
							1	P	R	O	P	E	R	T	Y
					2	R	E	F	I	N	E	D			
3	C	Y	B	E	R	C	R	I	M	E					
			4	B	U	L	L	Y	I	N	G				
								5	U	N	L	A	W	F	U	L
								6	C	O	L	L	A	R		
				7	R	E	G	U	L	A	T	I	O	N	
						8	V	I	O	L	E	N	T		
					9	J	U	D	G	E					
			10	S	T	E	A	L	I	N	G				
						11	I	N	S	U	L	T			
						12	D	E	T	E	C	T			

Solution: **criminologist**

Task 30

Statement	First four words
a) People have become more aware of the dangers of the web.	As the web's potential
b) Staying in touch with people presents less difficulty today than in the past.	Communication over the Internet
c) Criminals purchase in online shops using names and addresses of unsuspecting users.	The personal data can
d) Playing with the computer can be more dangerous than playing with other children.	They maintained that a
e) The Internet must not become a playground for criminals.	In the political arena

Hinweise:

a *"there has been an increasing recognition that the Internet can also serve as a powerful new medium for those who wish to commit unlawful acts." (ll. 3–5)*

b *"Communication over the Internet has now become easier than ever." (l. 16)*

c *"The personal data can then be used to order and pay for goods on the Internet." (ll. 23/24)*

d *"at greater risk of abuse sitting in a bedroom on a computer than outside on the street." (ll. 33–35)*

e *"avoid the Internet turning into a haven for unlawful activity." (ll. 55/56)*

Task 31

1. a) "maturation"
   meaning: **Matura / Reifeprüfung / to become older / mature / Erwachsen werden …**

   b) "challenge"
   meaning: **be challenging / competition / schwierig sein / Herausforderung …**

   c) "transforming"
   meaning: **Transformers / Transformator / umwandeln / verwandeln / to change …**

2. a) "maturation" (l. 55)
   - [x] development
   - [ ] extension
   - [ ] examination

   b) "challenge" (l. 46)
   - [ ] hard fight
   - [x] difficult task
   - [ ] serious offence

   c) "transforming" (l. 1)
   - [ ] extending
   - [ ] improving
   - [x] changing

   d) "recognition" (l. 4)
   - [ ] identification
   - [x] awareness
   - [ ] gratitude

   e) "disrupting" (l. 13)
   - [x] interrupting
   - [ ] destroying
   - [ ] altering

   f) "avail (oneself)" (l. 53)
   - [ ] pay for
   - [x] use
   - [ ] rely on

Task 32

0	1	2	3	4	5	6	7
A	D	F	H	G	E	C	J

Remember: There are no capital letters given at the beginning of each option even if it might be used as the introductory part of a sentence (e.g. gap 2). This will also be true in the "Matura".

Main Text (complete): Cyber Crime

The Internet is rapidly transforming the way we communicate, educate, and buy and sell goods and services **nationally and worldwide (A)**. As the web's potential to provide unparalleled benefits to society continues to expand, however, there has been an increasing recognition that the Internet can also serve as a powerful new medium for those who wish to commit unlawful acts. Every day **and around the clock (D)**, criminals are invading countless homes and offices – not by breaking open windows and doors, but by gaining access into laptops, personal computers and wireless devices using hacks and malicious software.

To cover these offences a new word was coined: cyber crime or wire fraud. Cyber crime is the latest addition to the group called "white-collar crimes" and represents one of the greatest threats to a country's national security, economic prosperity and public safety. Some hackers take down vital systems, disrupting and sometimes disabling the work of hospitals, banks and emergency services. **It is estimated that (F)** large amounts of money are needed to repair the systems hit by such attacks.

Communication over the Internet has now become easier than ever. With the rise **and the increasing usage (H)** of social network sites such as Facebook, Twitter and YouTube, Instagram and WhatsApp, people's ability to share photos and videos and exchange their personal thoughts and their political, religious and educational ideas with users all over the world **in real time (G)** is a simple click away. The negative side of the coin is that criminals breach social networks and steal the personal data of registered users. This unlawful activity is called identity theft. The personal data can then be used to order and pay for goods on the Internet. Therefore, warnings are issued to users of social network sites not to reveal too much personal data on their accounts. Social networking sites are not only misused for illicit activities such as theft, but also to cause fear in others **through threats and intimidation (E)**. As social networking is especially attractive and fascinating to young people who like to play games, have fun and keep in touch with friends, it can also become dangerous.

The office of the British Home Secretary has pointed to risks connected with the use of Facebook, Twitter and similar sites. They maintained that a child today could be at greater risk of abuse sitting in a bedroom on a computer than outside on the street. What they meant was that social networks are often used to be offensive or nasty towards other people. Cyber bullying or cyber abuse has become a widespread phenomenon and has caused concern among parents, **educators and politicians (C)**. Repetitive and persistent personal

attacks, insults and threats affect the victims of cyber bullying tremendously. There have been incidents of children thinking of hurting themselves because of bullying. Getting bullied on a social network is not only upsetting, it is also really hard to deal with. Anti-bullying experts offer help on how to reply to comments, remove tags, block and report someone to put a stop to the harassment. Criminologists agree that the rapidly increasing rate of cyber crime is a big problem and a challenge not only for private users, but also for governments and law enforcement agencies.
In view of the fact that the Internet is an important medium for commerce and communication both domestically and internationally, measures have to be adopted which ensure the safety and security of the web community. Home users are strongly advised to have an anti-virus programme installed on their computers or laptops **to provide protection against Internet fraud (J)**. In the business world, most firms avail themselves of the services of specialists to improve cyber security. In the political arena, politicians work out laws and regulations in order to guarantee the continued growth and maturation of this medium and avoid the Internet turning into a haven for unlawful activity.

Task 33

Statement	True	False	First four words
a) The Internet constantly offers new possibilities.	☒	☐	**As the web's potential**
b) Unfortunately, criminals take advantage of the enormous capabilities of the web.	☒	☐	**As the web's potential**
c) Crimes on the web have been committed for a long time.	☐	☒	**Cyber crime is the**
d) There are people who breach networks and destroy data.	☒	☐	**Some hackers take down**
e) Users are advised not to publish too many details about themselves and their families on the Net.	☒	☐	**Therefore, warnings are issued**
f) Teachers worry about the increasing number of threatening and intimidating messages.	☒	☐	**Cyber bullying or cyber**
g) Specialists can help effectively to stop people being abused.	☐	☒	**Getting bullied on a**

h) Official institutions and the police are more affected by cyber crime than private individuals.	☐	☒	**Criminologists agree that the**
i) Even computer programmes that detect malicious software cannot help much.	☐	☒	**Home users are strongly**

✎ *Hinweise:*

The line numbers given refer to the text version of the "Key" (pp. 104/105).

a *Finding synonyms can help you here: "the Internet" = "web"(l. 3); "to offer" = "to provide" (l. 3); "constantly [...] new" = "continues to expand" (ll. 3/4)*

b *Looking for paraphrases (expressing a term in other words) can also help. The phrase "those who [...] commit unlawful acts" (ll. 5/6) is paraphrased with the word "criminals", and "serve" (l. 5) is reworded as "take advantage of".*

c *In the text it says that "cyber crime is the latest addition" (l. 11). Therefore the statement is false.*

d *Follow the same procedure as in assignment b: Find the word in the text for which "people who breach networks" is a paraphrase, which is "hackers" (l. 13).*

e *The relevant words in the task sentence are "publish" and "details about themselves". A close reading of the text and searching for synonyms and/or paraphrases will lead you to "reveal" and "personal data" (l. 26).*

f *Similarly, the word "teachers" is used in the task statement as a synonym for "educators" (l. 38). "Threatening and intimidating messages" is the paraphrase or explanation of "cyber bullying" (l. 36).*

g *In the text it says that "it is also really hard to deal with" (ll. 41/42) bullying (the statement sentence uses the paraphrase "being abused"). Therefore, the statement is false.*

h *It is not true that "institutions and the police are more affected by cyber crime" because it says in the text that cyber crime is also "a big problem [...] for private users" (l. 45).*

i *The expression "computer programmes that detect malicious software" is a paraphrase for the term "anti-virus programme" used in the text (l. 50). As such a programme provides "protection against Internet fraud" (l. 51), it is – contrary to what the statement expresses – a real help.*

Topic 6: Obesity – a major health concern

Task 34

Y	B	W	F	A	O	V	E	R	W	E	I	G	H	T	X	U
E	K	X	F	T	S	T	H	W	A	C	W	R	K	N	B	P
Y	Q	W	U	R	P	R	O	M	O	T	E	V	S	D	S	E
H	L	S	F	V	Z	V	M	G	Z	W	G	U	P	I	T	R
G	I	Q	Q	O	J	S	D	Z	T	D	O	J	D	S	A	K
I	X	S	N	B	Q	W	J	L	Y	I	E	L	L	E	R	O
V	R	O	A	G	S	F	F	O	T	G	G	U	W	A	V	E
E	X	A	I	J	E	K	T	I	S	K	F	S	U	S	A	H
G	X	J	Z	H	C	V	R	B	B	M	O	Y	W	E	T	N
E	E	Z	C	U	M	T	Q	I	R	T	Y	S	J	E	I	D
T	F	X	L	B	U	F	A	A	Y	A	K	W	C	V	O	E
A	G	O	Q	N	E	W	H	I	W	K	J	U	Z	K	N	P
B	N	B	X	A	A	R	I	X	R	H	D	M	R	J	T	J
L	C	B	X	Y	S	O	M	K	R	E	E	L	R	B	P	R
E	Z	C	H	R	O	N	I	C	R	C	N	S	V	B	J	D
R	E	C	O	M	M	E	N	D	R	J	B	T	Q	D	Z	G
Y	K	P	V	I	E	X	H	K	W	I	F	O	X	E	S	B

Task 35

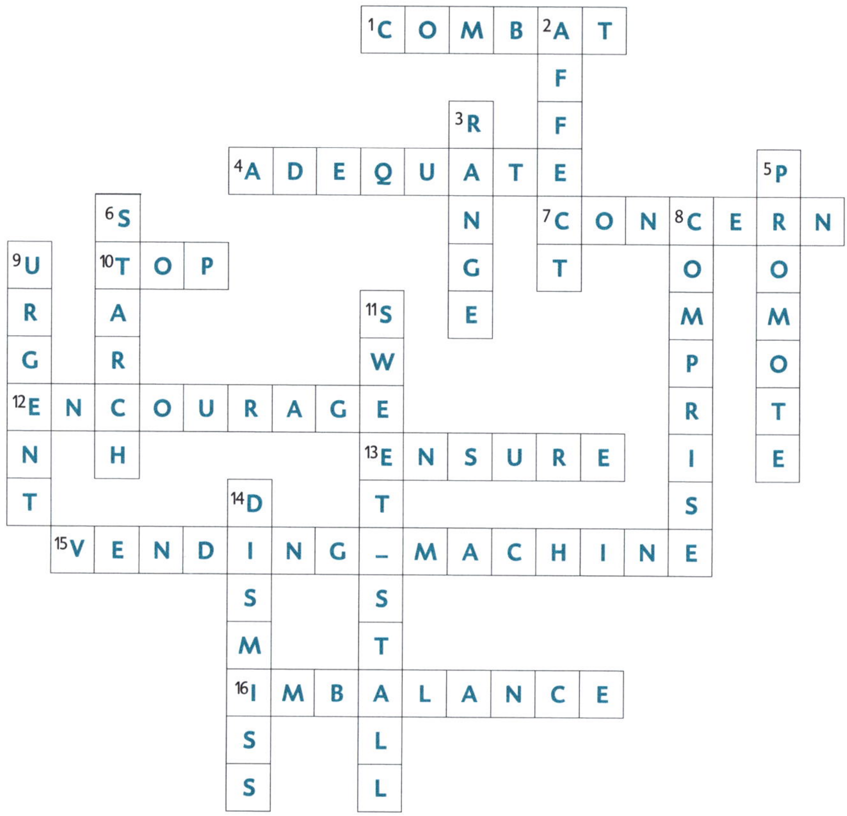

Task 36

Category	Weight (in kg)	BMI
underweight	less than 57 kg	below 18.5
normal	57–81 kg	18.5–24.9
overweight	82–99 kg	25–29.9
obese	more than 99 kg	30 or higher

The terms „obese“ and „overweight“ can sometimes appear as synonyms but here they show significantly different meanings.

Task 37

1. The text is mainly about obesity …
   a) ☐ in developing countries.
   b) ☐ in the USA and the UK.
   c) ☒ as a global problem.

The text informs the reader about obesity "in the United States and the United Kingdom" (l. 22), in "emerging economies" (l. 26) and also about other countries like "China and India" (l. 27), and the "Middle East and North Africa" (l. 29).

2. According to the text the number of obese people …
   a) ☐ has always been high in poorer countries.
   b) ☐ is declining in industrialised countries.
   c) ☒ is especially worrying in richer countries.

In the text it says that the "problem is particularly urgent in the richer countries." (ll. 21/22).

3. The author gives advice on …
   a) ☒ how to avoid obesity.
   b) ☐ how to take fast food chains to court.
   c) ☐ how to tackle the problem in emerging countries.

The text does not give any legal advice on how to take fast food chains to court ("verklagen"). It merely mentions the court case of two teenagers. Nor does it offer any information about how to tackle the problem in emerging countries. However, it does give advice on how obesity can be avoided by keeping to a healthy diet (cf. ll. 50–55).

Task 38

Country	Percentage of overweight or obese people
USA	70 %
UK	70 %
China	20 %
India	11 %
Middle East and North Africa	60 %

"In the United States and the United Kingdom 70 per cent of adults are either overweight or obese." (ll. 22/23); "in China and India, the percenttage of people

who are too fat has risen to 20 and 11 respectively." (ll. 27/28); "the Middle East and North Africa, where more than 60 per cent of adults are overweight or obese." (ll. 29/30).

Task 39

Statement	Line(s)
a) … Erfrischungsgetränke gehörten zu ihrer Grundnahrung	**ll. 5/6**
b) … verklagten das Schnell-Imbiss-Restaurant	**ll. 14/15**
c) … ist in den letzten drei Jahrzehnten plötzlich angestiegen	**ll. 19/20**
d) … ein Gesundheitsproblem in einigen Schwellenländern	**ll. 25/26**
e) … sind eher anfällig für schwaches Selbstwertgefühl	**ll. 35/36**
f) … war ihrer Gesundheit nicht zuträglich	**l. 65**

Hinweise:

a *"several soft soda drinks (= "Erfrischungsgetränke") were their staple (= food that is needed/used all the time) diet." (ll. 5/6)*

b *"took the fast food restaurant to court" (ll. 14/15); (to take sb to court = to sue sb)*

c *"The number of overweight and obese people in the world has surged (= has increased suddenly and fast) in the past three decades to more than 2 billion" (ll. 19/20).*

d *"overweight and obesity have become a health concern in a number of emerging economies (= "Schwellenländer")." (ll. 25/26)*

e *"Obese children are more prone to (= likely to suffer from) low self-esteem (= confidence in one's own abilities), negative body image (= a person's feelings about the attractiveness of their own body) and depression." (ll. 35/36)*

f *"eating so many fatty meals was not conducive to (= good for) their health." (l. 65)*

Task 40

a) Why were the girls diagnosed as obese?
BMI was too high
"their body mass index was much too high." (ll. 7/8)

b) When are people regarded as obese?
BMI 30 or higher
"Anybody with a BMI of 30 or higher is regarded as obese." (ll. 10/11)

c) What made obesity levels rocket in China and India?

fast food restaurants opened

"Since international fast food chains opened up branches in China and India, the percentage of people who are too fat has risen to 20 and 11 respectively." (ll. 27/28)

d) How did doctors traditionally explain people's overweight?

people are physically inactive

"For a long time physical inactivity has been regarded as the major reason for the increasing number of fat people." (ll. 37/38). This is the traditional, meaning "old", view. Lines 40/41 inform you about the real culprits: "sugary and fatty foods".

e) Why is the traditional explanation no longer valid?

many people practise sport

"more people practise some sort of sport today than ever before" (ll. 38/39). With more and more people being active (= practising sport) one would expect that the number of obese and overweight people would decrease. However, this is not the case. They eat more (and unhealthy) food than their body needs or uses up.

f) Why is eating several portions of fresh fruit and vegetables every day especially healthy?

supply micronutrients and vitamins

"this ensures an adequate supply of micronutrients like vitamins." (ll. 57/58) Fresh fruit and vegetables are rich in vitamins and minerals, and they are also low in calories.

Task 41

0. Two teenagers' parents sued a fast food restaurant because …

- a) ☐ the BMI of their children was too high.
- b) ☒ they held the restaurant responsible for their daughters' overweight.
- c) ☐ they wanted compensation for health costs.
- d) ☐ they were no longer served their favourite meals.

Option a is not correct because the girls' BMI was not the reason for the parents suing the restaurant but the fact that "it did not provide the necessary information about the health risks associated with its meals." (ll. 16/17). Option c is not correct because there is no reference that they had any costs, and option d is absolutely not true.

1. Obesity is an urgent problem …
   a) ☐ in South Africa and the Middle East.
   b) ☐ concerning mainly adults.
   c) ☐ concerning the younger generation.
   d) ☒ for young and old, rich and poor alike.

Option a is not correct, because the text does not mention South Africa. Options b and c are false because they limit the problem to one section of society only (b: adults, c: younger generation). However, in the text it says that "Obesity […] affects people of all ages and incomes." (ll. 18/19).

2. Obesity in younger children …
   a) ☐ has similar effects to smoking.
   b) ☐ leads to social isolation.
   c) ☒ has become more worrying than drug abuse.
   d) ☐ cannot be avoided today.

Option a is not correct because according to the text childhood obesity is worse than smoking because of its harmful effects on a child's physical and mental health: "growth and development, educational performance and avoidance of chronic disease throughout life. There are also psychological effects" (ll. 33–35). Option b is false because it does not say anything in the text about social isolation – although mental problems such as "low self-esteem, negative body image and depression" (l. 36) are mentioned. Option d is not correct because obesity can be avoided by eating healthily (see recommendations in ll. 50–58). There is proof in the text for option c, which is that childhood obesity has become more worrying than drug abuse ("No. 1 health concern", l. 31).

3. People put on too much weight because …
   a) ☐ they sit around instead of moving.
   b) ☐ they give in to the promises of advertising.
   c) ☐ food has become more sugary.
   d) ☒ they eat more than their body needs.

Option a is false because people are more active than ever ("more people practise some sort of sport today than ever before" ll. 38/39). Option b is also false because advertising is not referred to in the text. Option c only mentions sugar as being responsible for overweight and excludes the negative effect of eating fatty foods. Only option d gives the reason why people put on too much weight: "the imbalance between energy input (calories obtained from food) and energy output (calories expended in the basal metabolic rate and physical activity)" (ll. 45–47).

4. Nutritionists recommend that …
   - a) ☐ people eat mainly vegetables and leave out fat.
   - b) ☐ meals consist of mainly starchy foods.
   - c) ☒ people eat all sorts of food, but not in large quantities.
   - d) ☐ people eat small meals five or seven times a day.

The recommendations contained in the options a and b are false, because they are one-sided and therefore are not in line with the suggestion of nutritionists who favour a balanced diet. Option d is false: People should not eat five or seven times a day, but should "eat at least five or, even better, seven portions of fresh fruit and vegetables a day" (ll. 56/57). Only option c corresponds with what nutritionists really suggest.

5. The complaint of the parents of the two girls was unsuccessful because …
   - a) ☐ the judge did not believe their claims.
   - b) ☐ the restaurant presented evidence against the girls.
   - c) ☒ the judge ruled that the girls themselves were responsible.
   - d) ☐ the judge did not regard fast food as harmful.

There is no evidence for option a or for option b in the text. The judge did not voice an opinion about the effects of fast food as expressed in option d. As a matter of fact the judge told the girls that they themselves should have known better: "Common sense should have told them that eating so many fatty meals was not conducive to their health." (ll. 64/65). Therefore c is correct.

Listening Comprehension

Topic 7: Life in the UK – Citizenship Test

Transcript

T1

Life in the UK – Citizenship Test

PRESENTER: Life in the UK is an ambition for many and Salem is one of those people. Already happy in her own neighbourhood she's hoping to become a permanent citizen. To do this Salem and others like her will take the 'Life in the UK Citizenship Test'.

SALEM *(from Costa Rica)*: All my friends now are getting, you know, their citizenship and all these, and I'm left here and I'm thinking ... erm ... I'd just better do it now. I've been, you know, absorbing a lot of the ... Britishness. Yeah, I mean, my husband is British, and ... er ... my children are British, and ... erm, ... Yeah, I mean, I work here, I live here, I do a lot of things, ... er ... that British people do, so ... it's just the last ... the last thing. Is a lot of information. Yeah, and I think, some of that is ... easy, things that you learnt once you're, you know, here for a while ... but other things, I've no idea, you know.

PRESENTER: The test can be challenging and Salem is studying in the best possible way – with the official Home Office guide and study aids. *Life in the United Kingdom: A Journey to Citizenship* is the official handbook and has everything she'll need.

CAROLINE RUST *(Learning and development trainer)*: In my opinion, to use anything less than the official guide just doesn't make sense. To me it'd be like getting into a car being taught by somebody who wasn't qualified, or going to see a professional individual, a solicitor or a lawyer who wasn't qualified. It would be ridiculous.

SALEM: Definitely, to pass it, I have to ... to you know take some time and go through the book.

PRESENTER: Thea has just passed her test.

THEA *(from Fiji)*: It's very hard being a foreigner and this is written in English. You know ... you have to read more and do the practical. The more you practise, that's fine, it's fresh in your head ... go and sit the test.

CAROLINE: Facts and numbers are always tricky for people. There's no shortcut to learning. The bottom line is people have to focus and be dedicated to it, and there are some simple things that people need to do. They need to repeat what they're learning and try and learn in as many different ways as they can. Start off with subjects that are really easy, that they already understand. That would start to give them a sense of confidence.

THEA: You have to read it ... you know, carefully, I would say. Read the question carefully.

CAROLINE: It takes around seven seconds to really focus on a piece of information so that then you've got a chance to actually start it to be encoded, for want of a better word, into your mind.

THEA: Everyone was rushing to do the test; three minutes, the first time I did it in three minutes and left. But the second time I stay in for 25 minutes – the last one to leave the room ... and I passed.

PRESENTER: Jevin was born in South Africa. For him the test is the final step towards becoming a British citizen.

JEVIN *(from South Africa)*: I haven't had the time to get around to it ... erm ... I've seen the books, erm ... I've had a look at them. And it's basically, just finding the time to, ... erm ... to start revising and getting ready for the test.

CAROLINE: You've got lots of things to help you. There are CDs to actually put in your car so that you can listen as you're driving.

JEVIN: There's an app, with travelling around at least I've got it with me so I can revise for the test.

THEA: It's very helpful, the online now, ... the test ... because it's give you the answer instantly.

CAROLINE: Attitude is everything. Yes, there's some skill involved with this because people are going to have to have a skill to be able to learn. Yes, it was going to require lots of effort and determination. But if they think they can do it, they will.

JEVIN: When you come to the country ... and you involve yourself in it and you disassociate yourself and say, "I'm not different. Yes, I was born in another country, but this is the country that I want to live in" and you embrace ... er ... the British culture how things work in the country. You know, little things like when I first moved over I didn't have a clue what HRH stood for ... erm ..., but now, you know you, you get used to the acronyms you get used to what's going on in the country. You, you live it ... erm ... and I just find it quite exciting ... erm ... so I wouldn't ... I wouldn't be nervous. And I do ... I agree with what most people have said. Come into the country and embrace it ... and you'll enjoy it. I certainly have.

PRESENTER: To find out more including where your local test centre is, details on how the test is made fully accessible or to find out what support is available for those not familiar with computers, call the official helpline or visit the Life in the UK website. To find official resources and place an order, go to the TSO website or ask your high street bookshop for official Home Office Life in the UK publications. You can also join us on Facebook or follow us on Twitter.

From: The stationary office Ltd., https://www.youtube.com/watch?v=e2qqSNES-xl

Task 42 Possible solution: Foreigners living in the UK who want to become British citizens. / The government's idea to have a test for people who want to become British citizens.

Task 43 Some options are not topics of the real Citizenship Test: clothes, shopping, cars, football and cricket.
The others (law, geography, history, government, work, leisure, religion, statistics, education and health) are actually part of the test questions.

Task 44 The purpose of the text is to …

a) ☐ show how people from other countries live in the UK.
b) ☐ inform people that employers now require them to take the test.
c) ☒ promote interest in the test and encourage foreigners to take it.
d) ☐ explain that the test is necessary for foreigners wishing to live in the UK.

Task 45

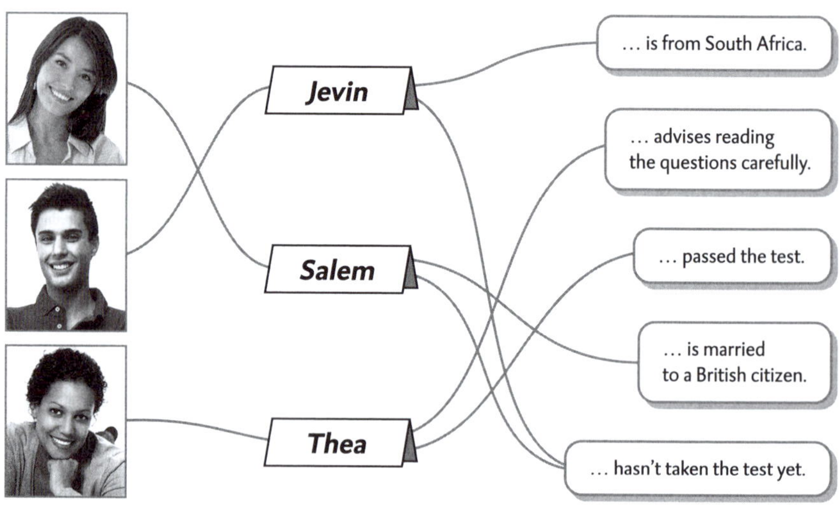

Hinweise:
Jevin: "Jevin was born in South Africa." (l. 43); "I haven't had the time to get around to it" (l. 45)
Salem: "my husband is British" (l. 8); "I'd just better do it now." (ll. 6/7)
Thea: "Read the questions carefully" (ll. 35/36); "... and I passed." (l. 42)

Task 46

0. Salem's decision was motivated by ...
   - a) ☐ moving to the UK.
   - b) ☐ getting married.
   - c) ☒ other people taking the test.
   - d) ☐ knowing the test was easy.

Salem says, "All my friends now are getting [...] their citizenship [...]. and I'm left here and I'm thinking [...] I'd just better do it now." (ll. 5–7).

1. The main advice is to ...
   - a) ☐ find a quiet place to study.
   - b) ☐ find out a lot of facts for yourself.
   - c) ☐ go to a qualified person for lessons.
   - d) ☒ use the government's material.

The presenter says, "Salem is studying in the best possible way – with the official Home Office guide and study aids. Life in the United Kingdom: A Journey to Citizenship *is the official handbook and has everything she'll need." (ll. 14–17). Also Caroline Rust says shortly afterwards, "In my opinion, to use anything less than the official guide just doesn't make sense." (ll. 18/19).*

2. One recommendation is to ...
   - a) ☒ begin with familiar areas to bring success.
   - b) ☐ learn the facts and figures initially.
   - c) ☐ take shortcuts whenever possible.
   - d) ☐ ask friends to help you learn.

Caroline Rust recommends, "Start off with subjects that are really easy, that they already understand. That would start to give them a sense of confidence." (ll. 33/34).

3. Thea probably failed the test initially because she …
   a) ☐ was not well prepared. b) ☐ wasn't really focused.
   c) ☒ did it too quickly. d) ☐ didn't have 25 minutes.

✐ *Thea says, "Everyone was rushing to do the test; three minutes, the first time I did it in three minutes and left. But the second time I stay in for 25 minutes – the last one to leave the room … and I passed." (ll. 40–42).*

4. People don't always have to …
   a) ☐ take the test to become a British citizen.
   b) ☒ study at home.
   c) ☐ take the online test first.
   d) ☐ practise the questions every day.

✐ *Caroline Rust says, "There are CDs to actually put in your car so that you can listen as you're driving." Also Jevin says, "There's an app, with travelling around at least I've got it with me so I can revise for the test." (ll. 48–51).*

5. People aiming for citizenship need …
   a) ☐ the ability to read and write well.
   b) ☐ to know they have a skill.
   c) ☐ special help.
   d) ☒ self-confidence.

✐ *Caroline Rust says, "Yes, it was going to require lots of effort and determination. But if they think they can do it, they will." (ll. 55–57).*

6. Jevin's experience is that to enjoy a country you …
   a) ☒ have to adopt its ways and become part of it.
   b) ☐ must forget the one you were born in.
   c) ☐ should find work and meet people.
   d) ☐ need to know the language first.

✐ *Jevin says, for example, "When you come to the country … and you involve yourself in it and you disassociate yourself and say, 'I'm not different.' […] Come into the country and embrace it … and you'll enjoy it." (ll. 58–67).*

7. Details about the test are …

   a) ☐ updated every year. b) ☐ difficult to find.

   c) ☐ only found on websites. d) ☒ not just online.

The presenter ends by saying, "call the official helpline" / "To find official resources and place an order, go to the TSO website or ask your high street bookshop" (ll. 70–72).

Topic 8: The hazards of overpopulation

The hazards of overpopulation – Getting to know the text

Transcript T 2

JOHN VIDAL: Since you wrote your books 20–30 years ago …

PAUL EHRLICH: 40 years ago.

JOHN VIDAL: Since you wrote your book 40 years ago, population has increased almost as much as you predicted. Have the environmental problems, er, followed exactly what you thought?

PAUL EHRLICH: Nothing follows exactly what you think. No scientist ever, 40 years later, would think the same thing they thought 40 years before in an active science but basically most of the things have gotten worse. The book that I wrote, er, was accurate on what happens in population, it was inaccurate in some other areas, but you gotta remember at that time, for example, I wrote about climate change but we thought that … we didn't know whether it was gonna be warming or cooling and we thought it was gonna be a problem for the end of this century. Now we know it's warming and it's a problem for the beginning of this century. We didn't know about ozone depletion, we didn't know about the loss of biodiversity. So, the things that have been coming up have been much worse than we predicted and that's what's got the scientific community scared.

From: John Vidal: Paul Ehrlich on depopulation: "We're over the top" – Audio, in: guardian.co.uk, 26 April 2012 http://www.guardian.co.uk/environment/audio/2012/apr/26/paul-ehrlich-depopulation-audio

The hazards of overpopulation

Transcript T 3

JOHN VIDAL: Since you wrote your books 20–30 years ago …

PAUL EHRLICH: 40 years ago.

JOHN VIDAL: Since you wrote your book 40 years ago, population has increased almost as much as you predicted. Have the environmental problems, er, followed exactly what you thought?

PAUL EHRLICH: Nothing follows exactly what you think. No scientist ever, 40 years later, would think the same thing they thought 40 years before in an active science but basically most of the things have gotten worse. The book that I wrote, er, was accurate on what happens in population, it was inaccurate in some other areas, but you gotta remember at that time, for example, I wrote about climate change but we thought that … we didn't know whether it was gonna be warming or cooling and we thought it was gonna be a problem for the end of this century. Now we know it's warming and it's a problem for the beginning of this century. We didn't know about ozone depletion, we didn't know about the loss of biodiversity. So, the things that have been coming up have been much worse than we predicted and that's what's got the scientific community scared.

JOHN VIDAL: Are you predicting more things like this to come up in the next 20 years?

PAUL EHRLICH: If we don't change our ways rapidly, then we're gonna have much more I think in the next 20 years, certainly in the next 40 years, er, but we're already seeing semi-catastrophic effects of climate change already.

JOHN VIDAL: We're talking about extremes of … of heat and cold.

PAUL EHRLICH: And tornados, and floods, and droughts, all of which are very serious for agriculture. Gotta remember all this is tied into our most important activity, which is growing food for ourselves, er, not trivial.

JOHN VIDAL: At the moment, do you see any way that the world can provide enough food … the carrying capacity of the world can provide enough food for the nine billion which they're expecting?

PAUL EHRLICH: Well, I'd say the first thing we ought to do is provide enough for the seven billion. We grow enough but the way we distribute it means that we have about a billion people hungry. And so we're gonna add two and a half billion people to that. They're gonna have to be fed from more marginal land with water that is transported further or purified more – in other words, we're gonna have disproportional impacts on how we can feed people from the increasing population itself.

JOHN VIDAL: Is that why you're saying the next two and a half billion people will be more of a problem, in a way, than the last two and a half billion people?

PAUL EHRLICH: Oh, yeah. It's always disproportionate because human beings are smart. We picked the low-hanging fruit first. We didn't start farming in marginal land and move to the river valleys, we did it the other way around – built cities in the river valleys and now using more and more marginal land.

JOHN VIDAL: But, we then come back to the next two and a half billion people who would be mostly born in very poor countries. Are you saying that … that the problem … is in fact the poor?

PAUL EHRLICH: Well, part of the problem is the way we divide up nations. Are, you know, are borders really moral? Or, we have very uneven distribution of resources over the planet. We ought to reorganize ourselves as a species, as Homo sapiens, and stop this poor world/rich world sort of thing. In the United States, for instance, er, people can live in quite natural areas and still have the benefits of products from industrial society. We could run the world that way, too. We just don't.

JOHN VIDAL: So, I mean, you're not in the business of predictions but if we go on at this pace ... and, er, and in this direction, what's gonna happen?

PAUL EHRLICH: There's gonna be various forms of disaster – they may be slow-motion disasters like just more and more people getting hungry, they may be catastrophic because the, er, the more people you have, the greater the chances of some weird virus transferring from an animal population into the human population – we could have vast die-offs there. We could have tremendous famines, again it's gonna depend a lot on the climate and what we do or don't do about it – how prepared we are for it, but I ... certainly have a grim view of what's likely to happen to my grandchildren and great-grandchildren.

JOHN VIDAL: But these are ecological statements, you're not making political statements. What you're saying is that it is inevitable that these ... the sort of event ... these extremes will happen from now on.

PAUL EHRLICH: Well, I think, that's now ... extremely likely. You gotta remember that politicians, for instance, can instantly change the financial mess the world is in ... that's something they have total control over, who's in debt to whom. But we, they don't have total control over – over the systems of the planet that provide us our food, that provide us our welfare in general. And those are deteriorating and it's going to take a long time to turn it around if we start now. We haven't started yet, so it's very hard to think of anything that's going to, in somehow, pop up and save us. I hope something does, but it would really be, er, you know, a miracle.

From: John Vidal: Paul Ehrlich on depopulation: "We're over the top" – Audio, in: guardian.co.uk, 26 April 2012 http://www.guardian.co.uk/environment/audio/2012/apr/26/paul-ehrlich-depopulation-audio

Task 48

a) ☐ The rising number of young and old people on the whole planet.
b) ☐ The risk of losing too many people from a country.
c) ☒ The danger that comes with the growing number of people.
d) ☐ The recent trend towards people living in cities.

Option a only refers to "overpopulation" (and not the "hazards" i. e. the "danger"), option b describes the opposite of the headline, and option d paraphrases the term "urbanization".

Task 49

a) One large concern is ozone **depletion** since the loss of this protective layer is responsible for climatic change. 1

b) A loss of bio**diversity** means having fewer animal species and plant types. 8

c) The land which is not ideal for growing crops is known as **marginal land**. 4

d) A **disproportional** impact is when the effects of something affect people in very different ways. 6

e) Hundreds of years ago plagues caused a huge number of **die-offs**, in some cases killing whole communities. 7

f) In his first year at the bank they only let him do the **trivial** jobs. 2

g) The result of our constant pollution of nature will lead to an **inevitable** catastrophe. 3

Task 50

a) Have the environmental problems followed **exactly** what you thought?
cf. ll. 4/5 in the transcript

b) The book that I wrote was **accurate** on what happens in population.
cf. ll. 8/9 in the transcript

c) We didn't know whether it [the climate] was gonna be **warming** or **cooling**.
cf. ll. 11/12 in the transcript

d) So, the things that have been coming up have been much worse than we **predicted**.
cf. ll. 15/16 in the transcript

Task 51

	True	False
a) A lot of information was unavailable when the book was written.	X	
b) Scientists are quite happy about current developments.		X
c) Everyone in the world could be fed.	X	
d) Cities originally developed where farming land was poor.		X
e) Paul Ehrlich dislikes the present situation of having rich and poor societies.	X	
f) Ehrlich believes that what we are doing today will benefit future generations.		X
g) Solving financial problems is not the same as solving environmental ones.	X	

Hinweise:

a *Paul Ehrlich says, "We didn't know about ozone depletion, we didn't know about the loss of biodiversity." (ll. 14/15).*

b *Paul Ehrlich says, "the things that have been coming up have been much worse than we predicted and that's what's got the scientific community scared." (ll. 15–17).*

c *Paul Ehrlich says, "the first thing we ought to do is to provide enough for the seven billion. We grow enough but the way we distribute it means that we have about a billion people hungry." (ll. 30–32).*

d *Paul Ehrlich says, "We didn't start farming in marginal land and move to the river valleys, we did it the other way around – built cities in the river valleys and now using more and more marginal land." (ll. 41–43).*

e *Paul Ehrlich says, "We ought to reorganize ourselves as a species, as Homo sapiens, and stop this poor world/rich world sort of thing." (ll. 49/50).*

f *Paul Ehrlich says, "I ... certainly have a grim view of what's likely to happen to my grandchildren and great-grandchildren." (ll. 62–64).*

g *Paul Ehrlich says, "You gotta remember that politicians [...] can instantly change the financial mess the world is in [...]. But [...] they don't have total control over – over the systems of the planet that provide us our food, that provide us our welfare in general." (ll. 68–72).*

Task 52

A	B	C	D	E	F	G	H
6	9	10	2	7	8	1	4

Hinweise:

A *Paul Ehrlich says, "The book that I wrote, er, was accurate on what happens in population" (ll. 8/9).*

B *Paul Ehrlich says, "at that time, for example, I wrote about climate change but we thought that … we didn't know whether it was gonna be warming or cooling and we thought it was gonna be a problem for the end of this century. Now we know it's warming and it's a problem for the beginning of this century." (ll. 10–14).*

C *Paul Ehrlich says, "And tornados, and floods, and droughts, all of which are very serious for agriculture. Gotta remember all this is tied into our most important activity, which is growing food for ourselves, er, not trivial." (ll. 24–26).*

D *Paul Ehrlich says, "I'd say the first thing we ought to do is provide enough for the seven billion. We grow enough but the way we distribute it means that we have about a billion people hungry." (ll. 30–32).*

E *Paul Ehrlich says, "We didn't start farming in marginal land and move to the river valleys, we did it the other way around – built cities in the river valleys and now using more and more marginal land." (ll. 41–43).*

F *Paul Ehrlich says, "We ought to reorganize ourselves as a species, as Homo sapiens, and stop this poor world/rich world sort of thing." (ll. 49/50).*

G *Paul Ehrlich says, "There's gonna be various forms of disaster […]. We could have tremendous famines […] I … certainly have a grim view of what's likely to happen to my grandchildren and great-grandchildren." (ll. 56–64).*

H *Paul Ehrlich says, "it's going to take a long time to turn it around if we start now. We haven't started yet, so it's very hard to think of anything that's going to, in somehow, pop up and save us. I hope something does, but it would really be, er, you know, a miracle." (ll. 73–76).*

Topic 9: Inside the White House: The kitchen garden

Inside the White House: The kitchen garden – Getting to know the text

Transcript
T 4

MICHELLE OBAMA: The garden was something that I'd always thought about. I was probably like most busy mothers, we were, you know, a busy working family – and I would find it difficult to feed my family in a healthy way, quickly. So I decided to change our diet and this happened throughout the course of the campaign and it was really simple things; adding more fruits and vegetables, trying to sit down as a family and prepare a meal a couple of times a week – eating out a little bit less, er, eliminating processed and sugary foods, erm, as much as possible. And I saw some really immediate results with just those minor changes. And I thought, well, if I could help other families, kind of learn these small changes in my role as First Lady, that would be a good thing.

From: The White House. URL: http://www.youtube.com/watch?v=aVpEr3kfWjc

Inside the White House: The kitchen garden

Transcript
T 5

MICHELLE OBAMA: The garden was something that I'd always thought about. I was probably like most busy mothers, we were, you know, a busy working family – and I would find it difficult to feed my family in a healthy way, quickly. So I decided to change our diet and this happened throughout the course of the campaign and it was really simple things; adding more fruits and vegetables, trying to sit down as a family and prepare a meal a couple of times a week – eating out a little bit less, er, eliminating processed and sugary foods, erm, as much as possible. And I saw some really immediate results with just those minor changes. And I thought, well, if I could help other families, kind of learn these small changes in my role as First Lady, that would be a good thing.

SAM KASS *(White House chef):* Today we are amending our soil and we've got our soil tested and it's actually in really good shape. So what we're gonna do is add a few amendments to increase the fertility of the soil, to, sort of, provide a lot of stability for the soil, er, and bring it into balance. Basically setting the foundation that we'll build on for years and years to come.

(Background voice: Ready, right now)

We're doing our first till, we're churning over the soil, er, about, we're going down about 6–8 inches deep and then we're gonna spread some amendments.

We're gonna use some sulphate of potash, which is basically just to add some sulphur. We have a crab meal, er, which is gonna add, er, er calcium, and, er, nitrogen – which is absolutely critical. And we use our crab resource from the Chesapeake, so we're all keeping it in the region.

TV ADVERT VICTORY GARDEN 1944: *Yes, what about me? No work, no spuds, no work, no turnip, no tank, no Flying Fortress, no victory. Bear that in mind all you victory gardeners and work for victory.*

SAM KASS: This is the first vegetable garden since Eleanor Roosevelt's victory garden in World War II. When we looked back at the records it was actually a really tough time getting it established and in the end it was a plot, you know, probably about the size of one bed that we have here, that one of the daughters of someone who worked here tended to. So as a sort of really productive, you know, feeding a lot of people garden, er, this is the first one in well over a hundred years. The seeds that we are using from, er, from Monticello that Thomas Jefferson had passed down were given to us by Peter Hatch, who's the head gardener at Monticello. Thomas Jefferson has more than any one man changed the way we eat, er, in this country and the way we, the way we grow food. When his ambassadors would go out all over the world, he would ask them to bring back seeds – and he's the first person to start seasonal growing. That is something that people are really, sort of, coming back to now and thinking about ways to, you know, use a diversity of crops and keep growing throughout the year.

MICHELLE OBAMA: People were, er, uniformly excited about trying to make this happen. Today is getting the soil ready and we'll come back in a couple of weeks to actually do the planting and then sometime in June, right … right around the time that school is over, hopefully we'll have lots of great vegetables and fruits. We'll harvest them and then we'll bring you guys into the kitchen in the White House.

SAM KASS: The … the kids from Bancroft who've helped us plant this garden have just been absolutely phenomenal.

MICHELLE OBAMA: Yes … Hey, look Sam! There's a carrot!

SAM KASS: … then came and gave these talks about what they've learnt. It was just mind-blowing – kids talked about … one kid talked about how she now eats all of her fruits … and all of her vegetables at dinner and her mom is noticing the difference, but that her favorite vegetable's carrots and just like people, I quote, "carrots have a history". The kids took this to a level that I could never have even imagined … they've just been tremendous.

MICHELLE OBAMA: We wanted the focus to be on kids because you can affect children's behaviour so much more easily than you can adults' and I saw that in my own life. My kids, you know, jumped on the new routine and didn't miss a beat and they began … began to monitor our behaviour, more so than I was monitoring theirs.

And also I wanted to encourage people to think about, erm, doing more family meals. We've found, er, that we've been able to do that and, you know, part of the message is, if the President of the United States can sit down with his family and have dinner, hopefully more families find the time to do the same thing.

From: The White House. URL: http://www.youtube.com/watch?v=aVpEr3kfWjc

Task 53

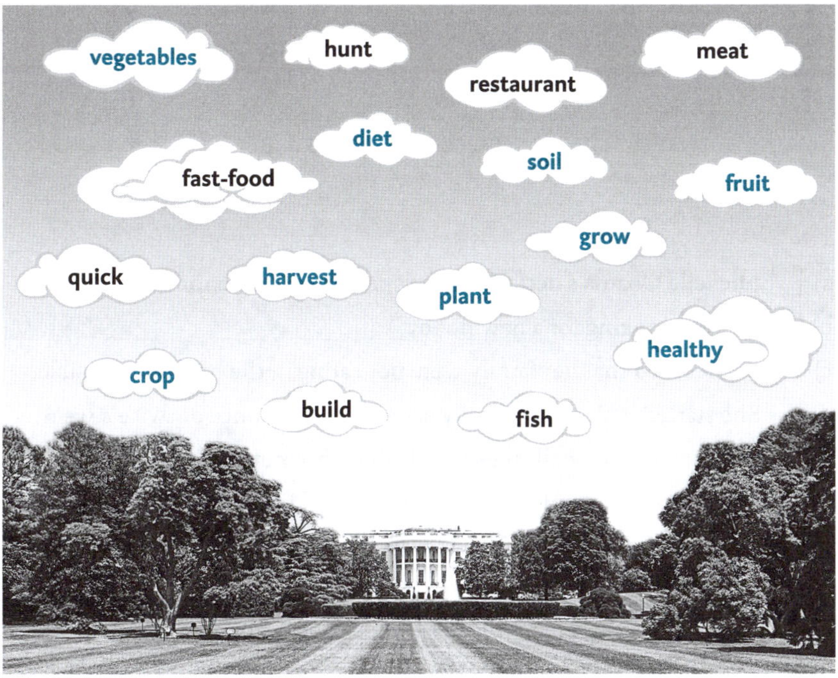

The words in colour here all belong to the overall topics "gardening" and "nutrition"/"food". Therefore, it is very likely that they might appear in the topic at hand. However, the given solution is merely a suggestion.

Task 54

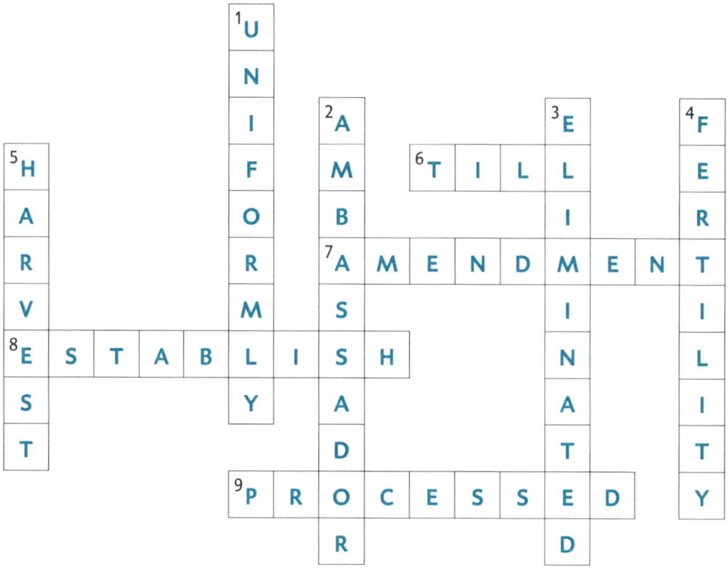

Task 55

a) ☐ Michelle Obama's decision was a spontaneous reaction.
b) ☐ She was looking for a new hobby.
c) ☒ She realised that her family were not eating in the best way possible.
d) ☐ She started making the family eat out together once or twice a week.
e) ☒ She took many small steps which all helped her goal.
f) ☒ She hoped she would become a role model for other families.
g) ☐ She believed a First Lady must play an active role in American society.

Hinweise:

c *Michelle Obama says, "I would find it difficult to feed my family in a healthy way, quickly. So I decided to change our diet" (ll. 3/4).*

e *Michelle Obama says, "and it was really simple things; adding more fruits and vegetables, trying to sit down as a family and prepare a meal a couple of times a week – eating out a little bit less, eliminating processed and sugary foods as much as possible. And I saw some really immediate results with just those minor changes." (ll. 5–9).*

f *Michelle Obama says, "And I thought, well, if I could help other families, kind of learn these small changes in my role as First Lady, that would be a good thing." (ll. 9–11).*

Task 56

	True	False
a) The recording is about the gardens of the White House.	☐	☒
b) Michelle Obama wanted her family to eat more healthily.	☒	☐
c) Her first task was to prepare an area of land.	☐	☒
d) It was the first time in more than 100 years that she'd created a large productive garden.	☐	☒
e) The first crops were expected in autumn.	☐	☒
f) The children were very excited by the project.	☒	☐

Hinweise:

a *It is not about the gardens but about a specific new one. (see headline)*

b *cf. ll. 3/4*

c *It was Sam Kass, the White House's chef, who was preparing the soil. (ll. 12/13)*

d *It was the first time in more than 100 years that a large productive garden was being created but it was not Michelle Obama who had created her first garden for 100 years. (cf. ll. 28–34)*

e *Michelle Obama says that the first fruits and vegetables will be ready in June. (ll. 45–47)*

f *cf. ll. 49–57*

Task 57

a) Michelle Obama thinks that she, her husband and the kids were **a busy working family**.

Michelle Obama says, "we were, you know, a busy working family." (ll. 2/3).

b) She just changed little things, but soon Mrs Obama could see **some (really) immediate results / the results (straight away)**.

Michelle Obama says, "And I saw some really immediate results with just those minor changes." (ll. 8/9).

c) The soil in the White House garden **needed some (a few) amendments / needed some (a few) additions / is basically good / is in good shape**.

Sam Kass says, "Today we are amending our soil and we've got our soil tested and it's actually in really good shape." (ll. 12/13).

d) The first gardening task is to increase the **fertility of the soil / soil's fertility**.

Sam Kass says, "So what we're gonna do is add a few amendments to increase the fertility of the soil." (ll. 13/14).

e) There hasn't been a large productive garden **for a long time / for over 100 years**.

Sam Kass says, "So as a sort of really productive, you know, feeding a lot of people garden, this is the first one in well over a hundred years." (Note: 'since Eleanor Roosevelt's' is wrong because it was not a large productive garden.) (cf. ll. 32–34)

f) Thomas Jefferson had a great influence on the **way we eat / way Americans eat / way people eat / way we grow food**.

Sam Kass says, "Thomas Jefferson has more than any one man changed the way we eat in this country and [...] the way we grow food." (ll. 36–38).

g) There is a trend these days that people think about **seasonal growing / seasonal fruit and vegetables / growing throughout the year / having diverse crops**.

Sam Kass says, "he's the first person to start seasonal growing. That is something that people are really, sort of, coming back to now and thinking about ways to, you know, use a diversity of crops and keep growing throughout the year." (ll. 39–42).

h) Sam Kass finds the pupils' enthusiasm to be **absolutely phenomenal / mind blowing / incredible / tremendous / amazing / totally unexpected**.

Sam Kass says, "The ... the kids [...] have just been absolutely phenomenal. [...] / mind-blowing / they've just been tremendous." (ll. 49–57).

i) It's easier to influence children's behaviour **than adults' / than that of adults**.

Michelle Obama says, "We wanted the focus to be on kids because you can affect children's behaviour so much more easily than you can adults' ..." (ll. 58/59).

j) President Obama eats **with his family / family meals / dinner with his family**.

Michelle Obama says, "if the President of the United States can sit down with his family and have dinner, hopefully more families find the time to do the same thing." (ll. 65–67).

Topic 10: How government influences behaviour in society

How government influences behaviour in society – Getting to know the text

Transcript T6

BARONESS NEUBERGER: Governments want to change our behaviour. That's what they do. They want us to get thinner, they're worried about obesity, they want us to use our cars less because they're worried about climate change, and a whole variety of other things. They want us to drink less – all sorts of things. And that's really one of the key things that governments do. So, how do they change our behaviour?

Well, this present government is particularly interested in what they call 'behavioural change interventions' that are relatively soft – they call them 'nudges', and that comes from two American behavioural scientists, Richard Thaler and Cass Sunstein, and what they say is you just change the default. So, for instance, we have rumble strips on the road and they make you slow down, or you change the design of a form and that makes you more likely, or less likely, to do something. Or, where for instance, in supermarkets, products are placed nudges you to be more likely, or slightly less likely to buy them.

From: Behaviour Change: a new report from the House of Lords Science and Technology Committee, June 14, 2011; www.youtube.com/watch?v=tPAAMazmmqU&list=PL99E082863E2F32D5&index=14

How government influences behaviour in society

Transcript T7

BARONESS NEUBERGER: Governments want to change our behaviour. That's what they do. They want us to get thinner, they're worried about obesity, they want us to use our cars less because they're worried about climate change, and a whole variety of other things. They want us to drink less – all sorts of things. And that's really one of the key things that governments do. So, how do they change our behaviour?

Well, this present government is particularly interested in what they call 'behavioural change interventions' that are relatively soft – they call them 'nudges', and that comes from two American behavioural scientists, Richard Thaler and Cass Sunstein, and what they say is you just change the default. So, for instance, we have rumble strips on the road and they make you slow down, or you change the design of a form and that makes you more likely, or less likely, to do something. Or, where for instance, in supermarkets, products are placed nudges you to be more likely, or slightly less likely to buy them. Those are nudges. And it was the present government's emphasis on using that kind of intervention rather than regulation or fiscal interventions that made us particularly keen to look at what's the science behind this – the behavioural psychology science, the behavioural economic science behind this, what do we really know about the science of changing people's behaviour.

The committee took evidence from about 70 people in person and then from about 150 people in writing, – organisations in writing. And we heard from a lot of experts, from psychologists, from economists, from advertising people, from supermarkets, from the alcohol industry and a variety of other people who have expertise. And we heard from people with very different views and we drew our conclusions from that. We also heard, if you like a fair amount of theory, and we had a specialist adviser who's a specialist in this kind of area.

The key finding of our inquiry is that nudges, these small behavioural interventions, on their own are very unlikely to give us a serious behaviour change in the population as a whole. And we came to the conclusion that actually government should look at using a whole array of interventions from these behavioural interventions to taxation to regulation to legislation and it's a package of measures that tend to help change people's behaviour and we know that so to some extent from previous experience like, for instance, people will remember with seat belts 'clunk, click, every trip' people remember as a slogan but there was legislation there as well. There was a campaign to persuade you, there were a whole variety of things all happening at the same time, which made it more likely that the population would change their behaviour – and indeed they did.

The committee hopes that the government will listen to its report, will read it with real interest and will take up some of our recommendations. Amongst the ones we hope that they will take up quickly are the appointment of an independent chief social scientist.

We were very surprised given the present government's emphasis on using these kinds of behavioural interventions that there isn't an independent chief social scientist in government. There are civil servants who are social scientists but we think if government is relying heavily on this kind of intervention, then independent advice into government is absolutely critical and we also think that an independent chief social scientist can, with the government's chief scientist, work with departments so that anything they do along these lines is properly evaluated so that government knows for the future. We hope that they will look at their behavioural interventions and this behavioural insights team at the Cabinet Office and we hope that they will look at putting those interventions together with other interventions to get a behaviour change, if you like, properly fixed in departments. We also hope that they will look again at the question of food labelling, which was an area where we had some very strong evidence from, amongst others, Justin King at Sainsbury's, to suggest that food labelling with a traffic light system – red, amber, green – is more effective in changing the public's behaviour in its shopping patterns than the present government's system, where you have percentages of recommended daily amounts and we were very struck by that because it was pretty clear that, in Sainsbury's anyway, shoppers were doing things in a different way as a result. And therefore we hope that the government will look at that one closely as it also looks at the voluntary agreements it's had, it's had with the food industry and the drinks industry and puts a time frame on them to see whether they've been effective and decides, if they've not been effective, to do other things as well.

From: Behaviour Change: a new report from the House of Lords Science and Technology Committee, June 14, 2011; www.youtube.com/watch?v=tPAAMazmmqU&list=PL99E082863E2F32D5&index=14

Task 58

There is no definite solultion to this task. However, the warning label on cigarette packs, as well as the tag on an electronic device showing its energy efficiency class, are classic examples of the government influencing our behaviour. The stop sign and the one stating "no entry" influence our behaviour but are rather signs of prohibition ("Verbote"). The other two ("40 % off" and the "exit" sign) should not be picked as they are usually not put up by the government.

Task 59

A	B	C	D	E	F	G	H	I
9	2	1	4	5	3	8	6	7

Translation of the example sentences:

A *Im Hörtext geht es darum, wie man verändert, wie Leute Dinge tun: dies wird oft als Verhaltensänderung bezeichnet.*

B *Manchmal ist ein Eingreifen in die Angelegenheiten anderer Staaten notwendig.*

C *Oft benötigen Menschen einen (kleinen) Anstoß, um sie daran zu erinnern, etwas zu tun.*

D *In Großbritannien gibt es viele Rüttelstreifen auf den Straßen, vor allem an Kreisverkehren.*

E *Die Finanzpolitik der Regierung wird von den Leuten nicht immer gemocht/geschätzt, da sie ihnen oft Geld kostet.*

F *Er weiß viel und teilt seine Fachkenntnis gerne (mit anderen).*

G *Die Regierung hat ein breites Spektrum an Möglichkeiten zur Auswahl./Die Regierung kann aus einem breiten Spektrum von Möglichkeiten wählen.*

H *Du musst den Brief der Frau persönlich geben.*

I *Ein Sozialwissenschaftler oder eine Sozialwissenschaftlerin ist jemand, der bzw. die sich ansieht, wie sich Menschen verhalten.*

Task 60 Governments want to **change** (l. 1) people's behaviour, for example, by getting them to use their **cars** (l. 3) less. They do this by something called nudges. Three examples of nudges are:

- rumble strips that make drivers **slow down** (l. 12),
- **forms** (cf. l. 12) which are altered to make people do something,
- and product placement in **supermarkets** (ll. 13/14) to persuade people to buy some things more than others.

Task 61 1. The government is concerned about …

a) ☒ people's weight and their alcohol consumption.
b) ☐ young people's drinking habits.
c) ☐ the health of older people.
d) ☐ living costs.

"Governments want to change our behaviour. […] they're worried about obesity. […] They want us to drink less" (ll. 1–4)

2. The concept of 'nudges' comes from …

a) ☐ the government itself.
b) ☐ economists.
c) ☒ some Americans.
d) ☐ psychologists.

"they call them 'nudges', and that comes from two American behavioural scientists" (ll. 8/9)

3. Nudges are preferred as an alternative to …
   a) ☐ fines and punishments.
   b) ☒ laws.
   c) ☐ official warnings.
   d) ☐ educational campaigns.

"Those are nudges. And it was the present government's emphasis on using that kind of intervention rather than <u>regulation</u> or fiscal interventions" (ll. 15–17).

4. Some slogans are very effective …
   a) ☐ to get people to change what they do.
   b) ☐ but only over a short time period.
   c) ☐ in changing people.
   d) ☒ because people remember them.

"people will remember with seat belts 'clunk, click, every trip' people remember as a slogan" (ll. 36/37)

5. The committee intends to …
   a) ☒ issue a report to the government.
   b) ☐ research the problem further.
   c) ☐ force the government to take action.
   d) ☐ demand change.

"The committee hopes that the government will <u>listen to its report, will read it</u> with real interest" (ll. 41/42).

6. Governments work together with …
   a) ☐ local people.
   b) ☒ various industries.
   c) ☐ supermarket chains.
   d) ☐ civil servants.

"we hope that the government will look at that one closely as it also looks at <u>the voluntary agreements it's had</u> […] <u>with the food industry and the drinks industry</u>" (ll. 64–66)

Task 62

A	B	C	D	E	F	G
5	8	2	9	4	6	7

Hinweise:

A *"Governments want to change our behaviour. That's what they do." (ll. 1/2)*

B *"'behavioural change interventions' that are relatively soft – they call them 'nudges', […] where for instance, in supermarkets, products are placed nudges you to be more likely, or slightly less likely to buy them." (ll. 8–15)*

C *The committee took evidence from about 70 people in person […]. And we heard from people with very different views" (ll. 21–26)*

D *"nudges […] on their own are very unlikely to give us a serious behaviour change […] we came to the conclusion that actually government should look at using a whole array of interventions" (ll. 29–32)*

E *"we know that so to some extent from previous experience like, for instance, people will remember with seat belts […] there was legislation there as well. […] the population would change their behaviour – and indeed they did." (ll. 35–40)*

F *"We were very surprised […] that there isn't an independent chief social scientist in government. […] then independent advice into government is absolutely critical" (ll. 45–49).*

G *"we had some very strong evidence […] that food labelling with a traffic light system – red, amber, green – is more effective […] than the present government's system" (ll. 58–61)*

Topic 11: Taking the thug out of thug life

Taking the thug out of thug life – Getting to know the text

Transcript
T8

FEMALE PRESENTER: Los Angeles has been called the United States' gang capital with hundreds of active criminal gangs. But the city is also home to a program that has helped thousands of young people say 'no' to gang life and to choose a better path.

MALE PRESENTER: As VOA L.A. reporter, Elizabeth Lee, told me, Homeboy Industries is so successful that other countries with gang problems are looking to it for help. Let's start with a look at her report.

ELIZABETH LEE: In what is considered neutral territory in a city of more than 450 gangs, 19-year-old Kevin is choosing to spend his days in a kitchen instead of the gang-infested streets of East Los Angeles.

KEVIN: Seen my best friend die. Seen all other family members dying 'cause of this gang life, you know. That's what opened me … opened my eyes.

MALE PRESENTER: Elizabeth, what struck me is that at this facility these are basically gang members trying to change their lives, but they are all coming from a different place and they are actually working together. So, what is actually making that possible?

ELIZABETH LEE: Well, the founder of Homeboy Industries, Father Gregory Boyle, explained it this way: he says it's hard to demonize someone you know. So, by putting these former rivals next to each other, forcing them to work side by side, eventually they have to start talking to … communicating with each other.

From: VOA Voice of America, http://www.voanews.com/media/video/1722334.html

Taking the thug out of thug life

Transcript
T9

FEMALE PRESENTER: Los Angeles has been called the United States' gang capital with hundreds of active criminal gangs. But the city is also home to a program that has helped thousands of young people say 'no' to gang life and to choose a better path.

MALE PRESENTER: As VOA L.A. reporter, Elizabeth Lee, told me, Homeboy Industries is so successful that other countries with gang problems are looking to it for help. Let's start with a look at her report.

ELIZABETH LEE: In what is considered neutral territory in a city of more than 450 gangs, 19-year-old Kevin is choosing to spend his days in a kitchen instead of the gang-infested streets of East Los Angeles.

KEVIN: Seen my best friend die. Seen all other family members dying 'cause of this gang life, you know. That's what opened me … opened my eyes.

MALE PRESENTER: Elizabeth, what struck me is that at this facility these are basically gang members trying to change their lives, but they are all coming from a different place and they are actually working together. So, what is actually making that possible?

ELIZABETH LEE: Well, the founder of Homeboy Industries, Father Gregory Boyle, explained it this way: he says it's hard to demonize someone you know. So, by putting these former rivals next to each other, forcing them to work side by side, eventually they have to start talking to … communicating with each other.

FEMALE PRESENTER: Many are working with former enemies.

KEVIN: As the time keeps going, you start saying 'Hi' to all male, 'What's up?' – you know – 'What's up? How's it going?' – you know. And at first, you know, you were shooting each other for a block, you were killing each other, killing each other's friends, you know. Just going … being rivals … to not … like, talking to each other. You know.

ELIZABETH LEE: And once you start talking to each other, then that's when there's healing.

MALE PRESENTER: Does it take a long time and is it … originally, start out, sort of rather stressful for them when they get there?

ELIZABETH LEE: The program that they go through at Homeboy Industries is 18 months. So, in that time frame, they start to get to know these people and start to break down a lot of barriers.

FEMALE PRESENTER: The founder of Homeboy Industries, Catholic priest Gregory Boyle, says former gang members can find common ground here.

GREG BOYLE: Everybody wants to feed their kids and pay their rent honestly and nobly. And everybody just wants their mom to be proud of them and their kids not to be ashamed.

MALE PRESENTER: Well, what specifically are these folks learning? What type of skills are they … are they acquiring?

ELIZABETH LEE: Erm … first they get education 'cause a lot of them have not finished high school. They also get on-the-job training skills; either in food service, as we saw with Kevin in a bakery, or … they also have a café, so they learn food service. They also learn other skills and also there's a tattoo removal service, so they can remove a lot of their gang-affiliated tattoos and that will help them get a job in the real world.

MALE PRESENTER: What is the gang life like in Los Angeles today?

ELIZABETH LEE: The gang life er … is the result of poverty and that hasn't changed in the last 25 years since Father Greg first started this program. And er … he says there are three main reasons why a youth would want to join … join a gang. First, it's just an … an utter despair in their life. They have no hope for the future. They can't even see past the next day and as a result they join the gang. The next reason would be someone who was traumatized and whether it's because of a dysfunctional home life or some other reason. And, thirdly, a … a smaller group are youth who are mentally ill. The … the basis for all this is extreme poverty. And there are many parts of Los Angeles that are still quite poor.

MALE PRESENTER: Is it hard for them to leave? In other words it can sometimes be dangerous for gang members to leave the gang.

ELIZABETH LEE: Father Greg says actually most of the gang members that he's worked with want a reason to leave the gang. And it's the community that originally had a hard time giving them a chance.

MALE PRESENTER: Well, what was it like for you covering a story like this? Being around gang members. Were you, sort of, uneasy? What was it like being around them?

ELIZABETH LEE: It was … it was a different feeling when I walked in, and the first thing I saw were tattoos. And not just tattoos on arms and … and legs but tattoos on faces and on necks, so it did initially make me slightly uncomfortable and realize that they may have this … kind of a scary image, but once you talk to them they … they sound, … they are just like, you know, … regular people. And then they smile, and they are courteous and polite. Erm … Kevin, the former gang member, told me that he feels more at peace and less stressed out now because he doesn't have to watch his back all the time. And he is removing his tattoos, just so he can start a new life.

MALE PRESENTER: And, er … Alex, last year, 8,000 former gang members went to Homeboy Industries and, as Elizabeth mentioned in her report, er … most of them do not go back to prison. So a very, very influential program. Our thanks again to reporter Elizabeth Lee.

From: VOA Voice of America, http://www.voanews.com/media/video/1722334.html

Task 63

a) ☐ Criminals leaving their street gangs by themselves.
b) ☐ Gang culture and how important it is in certain areas of Los Angeles.
c) ☒ An initiative helping members leave their gangs and that culture.
d) ☐ A government analysis of the gangs in downtown Los Angeles.

Task 64

a) Many gang members want to change **their way of life**.

b) Some people believe that they **have to behave / have to act / must behave / must act** in a certain way.

c) If you are by yourself, it's better to be safe and not to **walk alone at night**.

d) Frequently employers are not interested in giving **ex-convicts (ex-prisoners/former prisoners) work / former prisoners a job / ex-convicts a chance / ex-prisoners employment**.

e) **Appearance / How you look / How someone (a person) looks / Looking good / Someone's (A person's) image / Someone's (A person's) appearance** is just as important as someone's character for many people.

f) Many programmes **are/have become very successful** in what they are doing.

Task 65

A	B	C	D
3	6	4	2

Hinweise:
A *cf. ll. 5–7*
B *cf. ll. 9/10*
C *cf. l. 11*
D *cf. ll. 17/18*

Task 66

1. The programme in Los Angeles …
   a) ☐ started with hundreds of gangs.
   b) ☐ began because it is the gang capital of the world.
   c) ☒ has become a role model for other places.
   d) ☐ had difficulties initially.

The presenter says, "Homeboy Industries is so successful that other countries with gang problems are looking to it for help." (ll. 5–7).

2. Father Gregory Boyle's philosophy is to …
   - a) ☐ keep gangs apart so they take responsibility for their own territories.
   - b) ☒ make gang members mix by having them work together.
   - c) ☐ find work for gang members so they do not get bored.
   - d) ☐ encourage competition between rival gangs.

Elizabeth Lee says, "he says it's hard to demonize someone you know. So, by putting these former rivals next to each other, […] they have to start talking to … communicating with each other." (ll. 18–21).

3. Greg Boyle believes that every gang member basically wants to …
   - a) ☐ stay on the programme as long as possible.
   - b) ☐ be a success.
   - c) ☐ have a meaningful job.
   - d) ☒ have a normal life.

Greg Boyle says, "Everybody wants to feed their kids and pay their rent honestly and nobly. And everybody just wants their mom to be proud of them and their kids not to be ashamed." (ll. 37–39).

4. The programme aims to …
   - a) ☐ send people back to high school.
   - b) ☐ develop ex-gang members' social skills.
   - c) ☒ provide people with an education and work-related skills.
   - d) ☐ build up gang members' self-confidence.

Elizabeth Lee says, "first they get education […]. They also get on-the-job training skills" (ll. 42/43).

5. There are many reasons why people join gangs, however …
   - a) ☒ the main cause is poverty.
   - b) ☐ being in one provides a sense of security.
   - c) ☐ friends are the biggest influence.
   - d) ☐ having a 'cool' image and gaining respect are the most important.

Elizabeth Lee says, "The gang life er … is the result of poverty […]. The … the basis for all this is extreme poverty." (ll. 49–57).

6. Many gang members …
   a) ☐ have to become aggressive to survive.
   b) ☐ unfortunately return to crime after completing the programme.
   c) ☐ find their family and friends support them.
   d) ☒ would prefer not to be in one.

Elizabeth Lee says, "Father Greg says actually most of the gang members that he's worked with want a reason to leave the gang." (ll. 61/62).

Task 67 a) What is Los Angeles known as?
United States' gang capital

The presenter says, "Los Angeles has been called the United States' gang capital." (l. 1).

b) Why are other countries interested in the anti-gang programme?
it's (so) very successful / the programme is successful

The presenter says, "Homeboy Industries is so successful that other countries with gang problems are looking to it for help." (ll. 5–7).

c) Who did Kevin see killed?
his best friend / family members

Kevin says, "Seen my best friend die. Seen all other family members dying 'cause of this gang life, you know." (ll. 11/12).

d) What starts to break down during the 18 months of the programme?
a lot of barriers / many barriers / the barriers

Elizabeth Lee says, "So, in that time frame, they start to get to know these people and start to break down a lot of barriers." (ll. 33/34).

e) What can improve people's job prospects?
removing gang-affiliated tattoos / removing tattoos / removing gang tattoos / having (gang) tattoos removed

Elizabeth Lee says, "there's a tattoo removal service, so they can remove a lot of their gang-affiliated tattoos and that will help them get a job in the real world." (ll. 45–47).

f) When did the programme begin and by whom was it started?
when: **25 years ago**; by whom: **Father Greg / Gregory Boyle**

Elizabeth Lee says, "that hasn't changed in the last 25 years since Father Greg first started this program." (ll. 49/50).

g) Which factor is the most influential one making people join gangs?
extreme poverty / poverty / severe poverty
Elizabeth Lee says, "the basis for all this is extreme poverty." (l. 57).

h) What was the reporter's first reaction when she met the gang members?
she was slightly uncomfortable / she felt uncomfortable (scared) / she found them scary
Elizabeth Lee says, "it did initially make me slightly uncomfortable and realize that they may have this ... kind of a scary image" (ll. 69/70).

Topic 12: American icons: Georgia O'Keeffe's skull paintings

American icons: Georgia O'Keeffe's skull paintings – Getting to know the text

Transcript T10

KURT ANDERSON: She grew up on a Wisconsin dairy farm in the 1890s and taught school in Texas.

[...]

LISA MESSENGER: She was kind of having a nervous breakdown and I guess to bring herself out of it, she decided to accept an invitation to Taos, New Mexico.

[...]

GEORGIA O'KEEFFE: The sky is different. The stars are different. The wind is different. I shouldn't say too much about this because other people may get interested and I don't want them interested.

[...]

WANDA CORN: And she'd pick up rocks that she enjoyed or she'd started to notice bleached bones from animals that had been killed and left behind. So she'd pick up these bones and bring them home with her not knowing quite what she would do with them.

[...]

WANDA CORN: One critic wrote a very little review, but he just didn't even mention the bone paintings, as if he couldn't find a vocabulary that would put femaleness and bones together in some inherent way.

All from: "Georgia O'Keeffe's Skull Paintings" originally appeared on PRI's Studio 360.

Transcript

T 11

American icons: Georgia O'Keeffe's skull paintings – Part 1

KURT ANDERSON: This is Studio 360, I'm Kurt Anderson. Georgia O'Keeffe always considered herself a, a western woman. She grew up on a Wisconsin dairy farm in the 1890s and taught school in Texas. She never felt quite at home when she lived in New York City during the roaring twenties, even though she was a successful painter and had a famous artist husband, the photographer Alfred Stieglitz. Only in her forties did O'Keeffe discover the subject that defined her, the old animal bones that littered the deserts of New Mexico. She continued to paint them until she died at age 98. To understand why those sun-dried bones took such a hold on O'Keeffe and generations of her fans we will start with Lisa Messenger, who's a curator at the Metropolitan Museum of Art.

LISA MESSENGER: In 1929, Georgia O'Keeffe decides that her life is sort of falling apart, her marriage to Stieglitz is rocky, he's having affairs. She also felt, I think, just personally for her art that she'd lost her passion for what she was painting. She was kind of having a nervous breakdown and I guess to bring herself out of it, she decided to accept an invitation to Taos, New Mexico. And that was it, she went up. It turned her whole life around.

GEORGIA O'KEEFFE: As soon as I saw it, that was my country. I'd never seen anything like it before but it fitted to me exactly.

(Walking)

KURT ANDERSON: That's Georgia O'Keeffe speaking in a 1977 documentary.

GEORGIA O'KEEFFE: It's different. The sky is different. The stars are different. The wind is different. I shouldn't say too much about this because other people may get interested and I don't want them interested.

CAROL MERRILL: It's hard to look at New Mexico without seeing an O'Keeffe painting in every direction.

My name is Carol Merrill. I worked with Georgia O'Keeffe for seven years, from 1973 to 1979. And I was her caregiver, cook, nurse, companion, confidante. I would walk with her, talk with her.

There. That little building beyond is the O'Keeffe house.

I wrote her a letter and she answered the letter and her letter back to me said, "Dear Stranger," *(laughs)*. And, um, it was one sentence and it was, "Whenever you can find your way up here, let us know."

WANDA CORN: I'm Wanda Corn and I'm a historian of American art and I have a very special interest in the artists of the early 20th century, artists like Georgia O'Keeffe.

GEORGIA O'KEEFFE: I remember talking with a little girl when I was 12 and I said, "Lina what are you going to do when you grow up?" Well she didn't know. Well, I said, "I'm going to have be a painter."

American icons: Georgia O'Keeffe's skull paintings – Part 2

Transcript

T 12

WANDA CORN: O'Keeffe made her first trip in 1929 to Taos, and she got interested in property there. She began to go back to the same house … a small adobe house in a dude ranch called Ghost Ranch. And then she bought a hacienda in a little village called Abiquiu.

CAROL MERRILL: And on the windowsill, there would be all of these little rocks and shells and bones. And at some time I commented on how the bones made me think about dead stuff. And she said, "No, it … that was once alive".

WANDA CORN: O'Keeffe liked to walk in the desert. And she'd pick up rocks that she enjoyed or she'd started to notice bleached bones from animals that had been killed and left behind. So she'd pick up these bones and bring them home with her not knowing quite what she would do with them. So in the second summer she packed up a barrel in which she put some of the skulls that she'd picked up on the desert and she sent it to herself in Lake George, New York for the summer.

GEORGIA O'KEEFFE: That's where I began, that's where I painted my first skulls from this barrel of bone. At first I painted a horse's head. And then I got this cow's head. And I had the cow's head painted against the blue.

WANDA CORN: O'Keeffe's painting hangs in the Metropolitan Museum and it's called, "Cow Skull, Red, White and Blue."

LISA MESSENGER: It's a large, white, very rugged, chipped-looking cow skull smack in the middle of the painting.

WANDA CORN: With its two horns splayed out to the left and to the right.

LISA MESSENGER: There's a black band down the middle of the painting that I think really is probably the easel. And then in the middle it's blue, like … it looks kind of sky-like.

WANDA CORN: And then two red stripes, one on either side of the painting.

GEORGIA O'KEEFFE: And that was at the time that the men were all talking about the great American novel, the great American play, the great American, oh, it was the great American everything. And I thought they didn't know anything about America, a lot of them had never been across the Hudson. So I thought, I'll make my picture a red, white and blue. I'll make it an American painting.

WANDA CORN: When O'Keeffe showed the skull paintings for the first time, the audience for them was a New York audience. It was the same audience that she had been drawing for her flower painting for the last 10 years or so. And the critics discuss the flower paintings as if they could only come from a feminine gaze or speaker. And this became a little tiresome to her because she felt as if what she painted was always tied to her sexuality. And not at all thought, as male art was, as something coming from an independent spirit. One critic wrote a very little review, but he just didn't even mention the bone paintings, as if he couldn't find a vocabulary that would put femaleness and bones together in some inherent way. And somebody called them gruesome trophies in a sort of headline story and she wrote to one of her friends saying you know I'm just simply not doing what these critics say I'm doing. I'm trying to get a sense of place. I want to get some kind of sense, in other words, to give some kind of westernness to her work. [...]

From: "Georgia O'Keeffe's Skull Paintings" originally appeared on PRI's Studio 360.

Task 68

a) ☐ a person who has become famous and is very rich and influential

b) ☐ an era that is defined in a special way through style or a historical event

c) ☒ a person or object that has become a symbol of something and typifies it

d) ☐ an image or picture that everyone knows and instantly recognises

Task 69

1. O'Keeffe grew up on a <u>dairy</u> farm.

a) ☐

b) ☒

c) ☐

The best translation of "dairy" would be "Milchprodukte" in German.

2. She lived during the <u>roaring</u> twenties in New York.

☒ exciting

☐ boring

☐ expensive

The term "roaring" is often used in connection with the 1920s (German: "Goldene Zwanziger") and can be translated here with "wild"/"aufregend".

3. She had a rocky marriage.

a) ☐

b) ☐

c) ☒

The adjective derives from "(to) rock", which should help you to guess the context.

4. She had a good confidante who she could trust.

☒ friend

☐ horse

☐ dog

The word "confidante" means "Vertraute" in German.

5. She lived in a hacienda in New Mexico.

a) ☒

b) ☐

c) ☐

Picture b shows an "apartment building" and c shows some "terraced houses".

Task 70

0. At first O'Keeffe …

a) ☐ worked on a farm.

O'Keeffe grew up on a farm – she didn't work on one.

b) ☒ was a teacher.

She taught school (in Texas).

c) ☐ lived in Texas.

She worked in Texas but she was born ("grew up") in Wisconsin.

1. O'Keeffe went to New Mexico …
   a) ☐ to see friends in Taos.
   She accepted an invitation to Taos but it doesn't state who invited her.
   b) ☒ because of personal problems.
   "having a nervous breakdown" / "bring herself out of it"
   c) ☐ and received an invitation there.
   The invitation was given but it was before she arrived in New Mexico not after she had arrived.

2. She wanted to keep …
   a) ☐ people interested in the weather.
   She didn't want people to be interested in the area.
   b) ☐ everything different.
   Everything was different from what she had seen before, she doesn't express that she wants to keep it that way.
   c) ☒ the area a secret from other people.
   She says: "I don't want them interested"

3. Her collection of rocks and bones …
   a) ☐ help her to paint her pictures.
   Rocks and bones cannot help anyone paint a picture – they can be the motif but not the material used.
   b) ☐ were carefully selected.
   The rocks and bones were simply collected because she liked them, she had no plans to use them.
   c) ☒ had no initial purpose.
   "not knowing what she would do with them"

4. O'Keeffe would have been very happy …
   a) ☒ if the critic had written something about the bones.
   he didn't mention the bone paintings
   b) ☐ with the positive reviews of the critic.
   The critic wrote one 'very little review' and not 'reviews' nor was the review positive since it ignored her latest paintings.
   c) ☐ to have feminism recognised in her art.
   O'Keeffe suggests that the critic had a problem writing about the bone paintings because she was a woman: she would have been unhappy about this, not 'very happy'.

Task 71

A	B	C	D	E	F
5	3	6	7	2	1

Hinweise:
A *The presenter says, "She never felt quite at home when she lived in New York City during the roaring twenties" (ll. 3/4) – the 'roaring twenties' are the 1920s, which was a very exciting and fashionable decade.*
B *The presenter says, "Only in her forties did O'Keeffe discover the subject that defined her, the old animal bones that littered the deserts of New Mexico. She continued to paint them until she died at age 98." (ll. 6–8).*
C *Lisa Messenger says, "she decided to accept an invitation to Taos, New Mexico. And that was it, she went up. It turned her whole life around." (ll. 16/17).*
D *Georgia O'Keeffe says, "As soon as I saw it, that was my country. I'd never seen anything like it before but it fitted to me exactly." (ll. 18/19).*
E *Carol Merrill says, "It's hard to look at New Mexico without seeing an O'Keeffe painting in every direction." (ll. 25/26).*
F *Georgia O'Keeffe says, "I remember talking with a little girl when I was 12 and I said, 'Lina what are you going to do when you grow up?' Well she didn't know. Well, I said, 'I'm going to have be a painter.'" (ll. 37–39).*

Task 72

a) O'Keeffe viewed her collection of objects as things **that were once alive / that had lived / that weren't just dead**.
Carol Merrill says, "And on the windowsill, there would be all of these little rocks and shells and bones. And at some time I commented on how the bones

made me think about dead stuff. And she said, 'No, it … that was once alive'." (ll. 44–47).

b) Her first New Mexico inspired paintings came from the objects **she'd sent herself / that she'd found / she'd picked up / from the desert / in the barrel**.

Wanda Corn says, "O'Keeffe liked to walk in the desert. And she'd pick up rocks […] notice bleached bones from animals that had been killed […]. So she'd pick up these bones […]. So in the second summer she packed up a barrel in which she put some of the skulls that she'd picked up on the desert" (ll. 48–53) And O'Keeffe says, "That's where I began, that's where I painted my first skulls from this barrel of bone." (ll. 55/56).

c) Her first painting was of **a horse's head**.

O'Keeffe says, "At first I painted a horse's head." (l. 56).

d) O'Keeffe criticised many people for pretending to **know about America / be knowledgeable**.

O'Keeffe says, "And that was at the time that the men were all talking about the great American novel, the great American play, the great American, oh, it was the great American everything. And I thought they didn't know anything about America" (ll. 67–70).

e) She didn't like how the critics viewed her work on the basis of **(her) sexuality / her being a woman / her sex**.

Wanda Corn says, "And the critics discuss the flower paintings as if they could only come from a feminine gaze or speaker. And this became a little tiresome to her because she felt as if what she painted was always tied to her sexuality." (ll. 76–78).

f) In her work she was trying to achieve **a sense of place / some kind of sense / some kind of westernness**.

O'Keeffe says, "I'm trying to get a sense of place. I want to get some kind of sense, in other words, to give some kind of westernness to her work." (ll. 85/86).

Bildnachweis

S. 1: © Sam74100/Dreamstime.com
S. 4: Dmitry Melnikov. Shutterstock
S. 10: © Can Stock Photo Inc./Gl0ck
S. 13: Public Domain; http://pixabay.com/de/kinder-tv-fernsehen-home-menschen-403582/
S. 15: Aliaksei Smalenski. Shutterstock
S. 16: This image comes from the Project Gutenberg archives. This is an image that has come from a book or document for which the American copyright has expired and this image is in the public domain in the United States and possibly other countries.
S. 17: © Can Stock Photo Inc./lcswart
S. 19/S. 91: Imagemore Co., Ltd
S. 20: Stocksnapper. Shutterstock
S. 24: © Can Stock Photo Inc./marzolino
S. 25: LABELMAN. Shutterstock
S. 29: © Can Stock Photo Inc./cubrazol
S. 30: This work has been released into the public domain by its author, I, Jabberocky. This applies worldwide.
S. 34: Fer Gregory. Shutterstock
S. 35: **UFOs** © Can Stock Photo Inc./broukoid, **Kornfeld** This file is licensed under the Creative Commons Attribution-Share Alike 3.0 Unported license. Urheber: Arne Hückelheim
S. 38: Stephen VanHorn. Shutterstock
S. 39: © ivanmateev/iStockphoto
S. 40: David Evison. Shutterstock
S. 42: ene. Shutterstock
S. 44: Lightspring. Shutterstock
S. 46: michelaubryphoto. Shutterstock
S. 48: Warren Goldswain. Shutterstock
S. 51: marco mayer. Shutterstock
S. 53: © Can Stock Photo Inc./Andres
S. 59: © Can Stock Photo Inc./yurkaimmortal
S. 60/S. 116: **Frau (oben)** Andresr. Shutterstock, **Mann** © Lucabertolli/Dreamstime.com, **Frau (unten)** Christine Langer-Pueschel. Shutterstock
S. 61: © Can Stock Photo Inc./hypermania
S. 62: © Can Stock Photo Inc./michaklootwijk
S. 63: ALLERIM. Shutterstock
S. 64: © Can Stock Photo Inc./RCarner
S. 66/S. 127: Diese Datei ist unter der Creative-Commons-Lizenz „Namensnennung – Weitergabe unter gleichen Bedingungen 3.0 nicht portiert" lizenziert. Fotograf: Daniel Schwen
S. 67: © Katrina Brown/Dreamstime.com
S. 68: Urheberrecht bei der U.S.-Regierung; Children from Bancroft Elementary School in Washington, D.C. help First Lady Michelle Obama plant the White House Vegetable Garden, April 9, 2009. (Official White House Photo by Samantha Appleton)
S. 70: **Schild No Entry** © TACLUDA/RGBstock, **Stoppschild** Public Domain: http://commons.wikimedia.org/wiki/File:Stop_sign_at_sunset.jpg?uselang=de, **Waschmaschine** © Can Stock Photo Inc./ironjohn, **Schild 40%** © RWLinder/RGBstock, **Gesundheitswarnung** Public Domain; Urheber: CDC/Debora Cartagena, **Schild Exit** Diese Datei ist unter der Creative-Commons-Lizenz „Namensnennung – Weitergabe unter gleichen Bedingungen 3.0 nicht portiert" lizenziert. Urheber: Gazebo
S. 71: Prapann. Shutterstock
S. 72: robin2. Shutterstock
S. 73: **Stempel Sugar Free** © Can Stock Photo Inc./aquir, **Labels** © Can Stock Photo Inc./Orson
S. 76: **Junge Graffiti** Nejron Photo. Shutterstock, **Mikrofon** © Can Stock Photo Inc./wellphoto, **Pistole** © Can Stock Photo Inc./Mark2121
S. 77: © Ozzon/Dreamstime.com
S. 79/S. 146: **Weizen** Repina Valeriya. Shutterstock, **Milchprodukte** Valentyn Volkov. Shutterstock, **Schinken** MaraZe. Shutterstock

S. 80/S. 147: **Hazienda** This file is licensed under the Creative Commons Attribution-Share Alike 4.0 International, 3.0 Unported, 2.5 Generic, 2.0 Generic and 1.0 Generic license. Urheber: Santi-sinaloa, **Hochhaus** © RWLinder/RGBstock, **Reihenhäuser** r.nagy. Shutterstock
S. 82: Library of Congress, Prints and Photographs Division, Van Vechten Collection
S. 83: Dimitri Castrique Ploegsteert
S. 85: Sven Hoppe. Shutterstock

Erfolgreich durch alle Klassen und die Matura mit den STARK-Reihen

Zentral-Matura

Mit kompetenzorientierten Aufgaben im Stil der schriftlichen Zentralmatura. Dazu ausführliche, kommentierte Lösungen.

Matura-Training

Prüfungsrelevantes Wissen schülergerecht präsentiert. Übungsaufgaben mit Lösungen sichern den Lernerfolg.

STARK in Schularbeiten

Themenbezogen und nachhaltig Wissen sichern. Mit Tests zur Selbstüberprüfung.

Kompakt-Wissen

Kompakte Darstellung des prüfungsrelevanten Wissens zum schnellen Nachschlagen und Wiederholen.

Sprachenzertifikate

Gezielte Vorbereitung auf Prüfungen wie KET/telc A2 und PET/telc B1.

Und vieles mehr auf www.stark-verlag.at

(Bitte blättern Sie um)